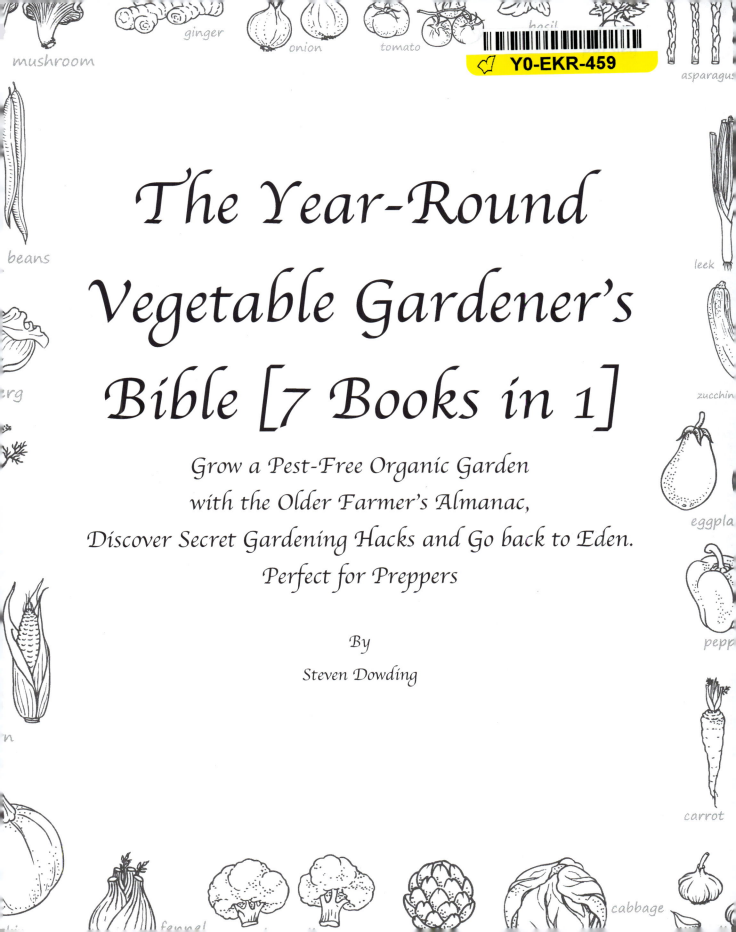

The Year-Round Vegetable Gardener's Bible [7 Books in 1]

Grow a Pest-Free Organic Garden
with the Older Farmer's Almanac,
Discover Secret Gardening Hacks and Go back to Eden.
Perfect for Preppers

By

Steven Dowding

mushroom

ginger

onion

tomato

basil

parsley

asparagus

ABOUT THE AUTHOR

leek

zucchini

beans

S teven Dowding is the owner of an organic farm near Mason City (Iowa). He cultivates his own garden, intending to safeguard heirloom seeds from extinction, ancient varieties of vegetables resistant to diseases and endowed with good nutritional properties. He has been a seed saver for almost 25 years now.

It was January 1996, and while it was raining outside, he was bored leafing through the catalogs of the seed companies that he had found one after the other. Determined to order seeds for spring, Steven found these catalogs very similar, with the same varieties of vegetables, tomatoes, carrots, peppers, zucchinis, and eggplants; the names changed, but the shapes and colors were always the same.

eggpla

So, Steven decided to go to the countryside, looking for something different. He abandoned the city and his previous activity as a herbalist. He chose to live and work full-time as an organic farmer and seed saver, trying to implement a project for a family garden that would ensure him and his family good food self-sufficiency.

Steven is a vegetarian, and he makes sure to have on his table not only vegetables and fruits obtained without the use of pesticides but also the flavors, aromas, and fragrances that no longer inhabit modern farm products.

pepp

Steven is also a book writer; he constantly connects with seed saving networks across the United States, widening his searches by sending letters to look for seeds suitable for organic farming. As a pro seed saver, he is convinced that the plants he would obtain from sources produced with organic methods would be stronger and more resistant to disease.

Steven lives in Iowa with his family and his dog, Buck, who also helps him grow seeds!

carrot

fennel

cabbage

TABLE OF CONTENTS

garlic

zucchini

mushroom

artichoke

pepper

tomato

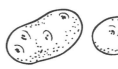

potato

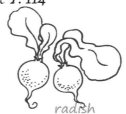

radish

cabbage

onion   *carrot*

leek

fennel

cauliflower

INTRODUCTION

Once it was said that agriculture was a tiring and not very noble profession, they used to say: "The land is low!" Today the situation has unexpectedly reversed: a handkerchief of land to cultivate has become a kind of status symbol.

It is an enormous pleasure to hear friends, acquaintances, and an ever-increasing number of people get excited about having managed to grow tomatoes on the balcony or for having given new life to the kitchen garden in the countryside.

It is truly a period of a cultural renaissance. While consumption models fail, while the economic crisis is raging, people react by going back to doing something concrete and useful for mental and physical health.

As if to say that even if the world around us collapses, there is always a little hope in cultivating our little garden and in realizing that it takes very little to be happy.

Alone or with your family: growing crops and vegetable gardens are becoming a way to save relationships between people; in some cases, it's better than a holiday.

Obviously, the earth has always remained 'low-lying' and always requires effort, but it is certainly a form of physical effort that, if done right, regenerates the body and mind.

I like the vision of the Japanese, who are much more farsighted than us in this sense. As a dear friend who went to live in Japan told me, in those parts, it is customary to say: working the land is the noblest profession, as it is the only case in which one must often kneel without ever losing one's honor.

But if the garden is good for the wellness of citizens and can be a choice of taste, it can also represent the solution to even more serious problems, such as poverty.

According to the FAO, by 2020, the global urban population living in extreme poverty could reach 45 % or 1.4 billion people.

Faced with this so-called 'population bomb,' the best detonator for FAO consists in picking up the hoes and cultivating in the city and in the peri-urban countryside.

In Africa alone, there are 130 million urban farmers, and in Latin America, 230 million. Shivaji Pandey, director of FAO's Crop Production and Plant Protection Division, says urban horticulture is the solution to the problem of poverty: it's the cheapest way to access fresh food with the best organoleptic qualities.

The cheap urban food consumed by the poor population is of poor quality: it has a high fat and sugar content and is responsible for chronic diseases such as diabetes and cardiovascular diseases. Especially in poorer urban areas, there is less and less fresh quality food available.

This phenomenon, characteristic above all of the large cities, is called the 'food desert' and indicates the areas of the city where there is a recognized difficulty in accessing food.

From the North to the South of the world, the garden, therefore, becomes the way to defeat poverty and the economic crisis, to get by on your own, to be outdoors, and why not?, to learn again to take the right measure of time, the seasons and the beauty of simple things.

The vegetable garden, then, becomes important for understanding, from an early age, the origin of food, the way to produce it yourself, increasing food security, and creating a healthier environment and community.

It helps to reduce energy consumption and waste production, reduce waste and increase the quality of life.

According to the sociologist Kaplan, if we cultivate to obtain a harvest, we use voluntary attention oriented towards the achievement of a goal.

So, thanks to four aspects highlighted by Kaplan, I discovered 4 emblematic keywords I want to pass to you that represent the secret of the powerful vegetable garden to reduce daily stress:

- Being away: understood as «distraction,» distance from problems. When we are immersed in a natural environment, we distance ourselves from the contingent, from the anguish of everyday life.
- Fascination: understood as «enchantment.» This concept is closely connected to that of beauty, that is to say to that wonder and seduction that make us use the involuntary attention that acts without cerebral effort and in the stillness of the mind.
- Extent: encompasses the concept of spatiality, interpenetration, and «connection.» It is

the aspect linked to biophilia and our belonging to one or more connected systems.

- Compatibility: understood as 'affinity,' feeling at ease. And it indicates exactly what happens in a garden, where defenses are abandoned: we don't feel judged and we don't judge, we don't feel separate, and we don't separate, we don't feel offended, and we don't offend.

The vegetable garden is the ideal scenario in which to heal the discomforts of body and soul.

Cultivating can give you a second chance; it can be the way and the opportunity to regain your life back.

The garden thus becomes a tool to improve everyone's life, and, thanks to its simplicity, it is the keystone for the care of people and the community.

This is what the treasure of this great cultural, sustainable, and love for ourselves and our planet phenomenon consists of:

- **BOOK 1: Vegetable Gardening History | The Journey Begins**: Go Back to Basics, Learn from the Past to Improve the Future, and Be the Next Vegetable Gardener's Master.

- **BOOK 2: The Vegetable Gardener's Pest Handbook:** Discover 9+1 Organic and Affordable Ways to Grow and Maintain Your Pest-Free Garden 365 Days a Year.

- **BOOK 3: Vegetable Gardening Hacks:** Vertical, Balcony, Shady, Container, Small-Scale, Raised Bed, Veggie, No-Dig Hydroponic Vegetable Gardening, High Yielding Wall, Wide Rows, Deep Soil, Companion Planting.

- **BOOK 4: Vegetable Gardening for Modern Preppers:** Create Your Own Doomsday-Proof Garden & Learn how to Harvest, Grow and Store Vegetables to Build Your Time-Proof Long Term Pantry.

- **BOOK 5: The Self-Sufficient Backyard Homestead:** Start Your Organic Mini-Farm with a Perfect Layout, Following the Old Farmer's Almanac.

- **BOOK 6: The Seed Saving Handbook:** Harvest, Store, Germinate and Keep Vegetables, Plants, Fruits and Herbs Fresh for 5+ Years, Build Your Own Seed Bank & Live the Frugal Gardening Lifestyle.

- **BOOK 7: Make Money with Excess Vegetables:** Sell Surplus Vegetables, Monetize Your Hard Work, Build an Additional Stream of Income, and Make Infinite ROI.

Are you ready to dig in?

Let's go!

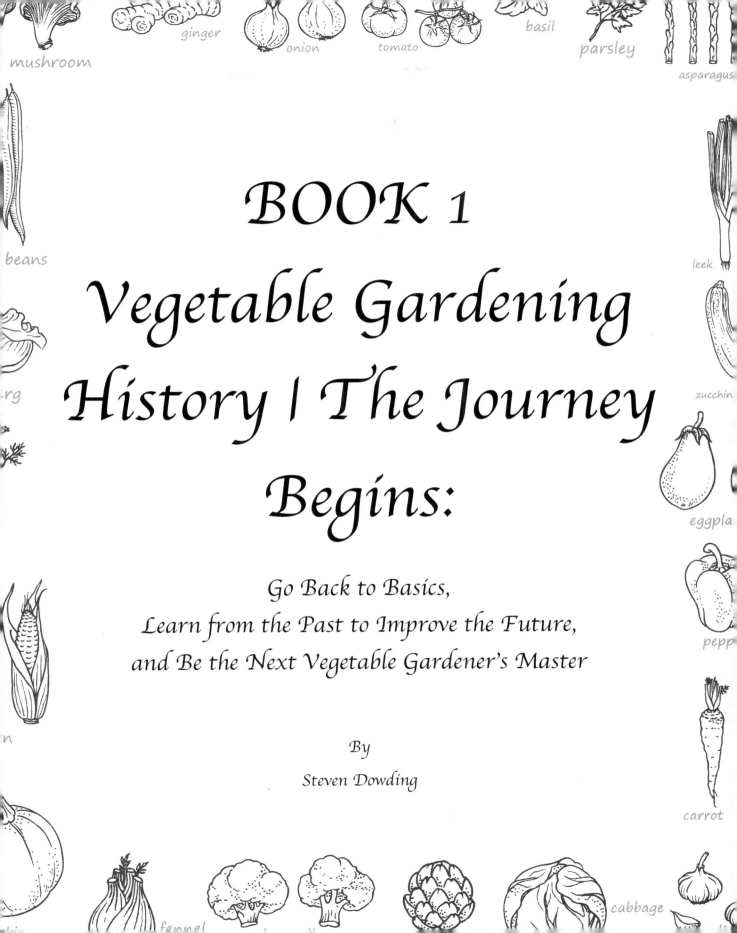

BOOK 1

Vegetable Gardening History | The Journey Begins:

Go Back to Basics,
Learn from the Past to Improve the Future,
and Be the Next Vegetable Gardener's Master

By

Steven Dowding

Chapter 1.

AMERICA'S FIRST FORM OF SLAVERY

G *rowing your own food should be a basic skill, like breathing or brushing your teeth. Every child with their hands on the Earth is changing their life and the whole world.* These are the words of Ron Finley - America's most famous eco-gardener - from a place in Los Angeles that we could define as a garden, vegetable garden, or jungle: it is the courtyard where he started his urban agricultural rebellion in 2010.

Finley speaks with the pride of someone who started a revolution in the desert: transforming the desolation of the most desperate neighborhoods of L.A. in a sequence of community gardens, where food is never just food but a liberation movement.

Ron is a friend of the actress, Rosario Dawson. He appeared in American Vogue and holds prestigious online masterclasses, but when he talks about himself, surrounded by his plants, the glamorous patina comes off immediately: he willingly mentions anti-system movements such as the Black Panthers, and the word he uses most often is revolution. The gardens he created and the ones he inspired in this decade with his lessons are a way to change America, the same as school shootings, gangs, and the police killing black people like him. *'You can't be free if you can't feed yourself: food is America's first form of slavery.'*

As he teaches families and kids in Los Angeles' Black and Latino communities to compost, Ron

STEVEN DOWDING | THE YEAR-ROUND VEGETABLE GARDENER'S BIBLE [7 BOOKS IN 1]

fights not only poor nutrition but also systemic racism. It is the same battle started in the White House by Michelle Obama. Both knew that, before Martin Luther King, racial segregation was in schools and on buses, but today it's in supermarkets and on plates. South Central and Beverly Hills are less than ten kilometers apart, but in his poor, black neighborhood, obesity rates are five times higher. Those gardens are a vegetable class struggle.

Without necessarily wanting to fight against years of history, just think of how much value and how much power is hidden behind the cultivation of a vegetable garden, an act that gives us practical sustenance - eating - and also reconnects us with the sense of human history on the Earth.

He called it «gangsta gardening,» homage and bio evolution of gangsta rap. Gardening for gangsters. Which is gardening, as always, just with a little more arrogance. Another of the phrases with which he convinces young people to devote their time to the land is that planting seeds is like growing your own money.

Twelve years after the first seed, today, Ron does what he has done more or less every day for the last decade: he wakes up early. He plants, sows, weeds, and tills. In addition, however, he travels the world, meets companies and politicians, and holds conferences at universities.

The pandemic amplified his message: people were locked up at home and looking for meaning, a road, something to look forward to, and he had one or two suggestions. *'Sometimes I can't believe the impact my gardens have had. This morning a guy wrote to me to tell me that after listening to me and starting to grow vegetables, he too returned to talk to him, his mother, after so many years'*. With his friend Rosario Dawson, he shot a video to promote regenerative agriculture through climate victory gardens. It is a reminder of the 20 million victory gardens created by the Americans during the world wars to send more food to the troops on the front lines. But the center of his life remains the Ron Finley Project, the community work to replace concrete and asphalt in Los Angeles with cultivated fields.

What does this experience teach us? How much value it has not only to think and build a personalized garden and grow vegetables but also to understand how it can save our lives in a world facing serious problems, which always include a good dose of food shortage.

This a concept that first preppers and then seed savers around the world have embraced and spread for years now, also contributing to the growth of an ever more fundamental awareness.

On the other hand, learning to work vegetables has a very ancient history. Let's discover it!

Chapter 2.
FROM AGRICULTURE
TO VEGETABLE GARDENS

The birth of agriculture can be traced back to about 10,000 years ago in the so-called Fertile Crescent. Before then, man practiced hunting animals and gathering the berries, roots, and fruits of plants that were born spontaneously on the ground.

From that moment, man began to cultivate plants and raise livestock. From nomads, they became sedentary; they were permanently linked to the land and built the first villages. The first tools for working the land were pointed and fire-hardened tree branches, stones, and sharp bones with which to reap the crop.

The first plow was built around 3500 BC. At first, it was pulled by hand, later by oxen. The plow was perfected around 1000 BC, replacing its wooden tip with an iron one, which made it possible to cultivate harder and more compact soils. The construction of millstone and later water mills allowed man to process large quantities of cereals.

The application of some new agricultural techniques, such as land irrigation and crop rotation, allowed man to improve the quality of the products. With the Roman expansion, moreover, the work of the land passed to slaves, as the peasants gradually abandoned the countryside to move to the cities. Thus began the decline of agriculture, accentuated by the barbarian invasions.

Only after 1000 AD. agriculture began to flourish again. In this period, important innovations were introduced, such as the rigid collar and the shoeing of the horses' hooves, to increase the pulling power and the wheeled plough.

With the discovery of America, new edible plants and animals were introduced to Europe. Agricultural machinery was introduced in the eighteenth century. The first grain seeders and threshers represented the transition from the use of energy to that of mechanical energy. All this made it possible to significantly increase production but saw a progressive decrease in agricultural workers.

In the nineteenth century, agricultural sciences developed, which gave a great impulse to the creation of the first chemical fertilizers and herbicides. The spread of the tractor further accelerated the mechanization of agriculture. Unfortunately, the last thirty years of the twentieth century saw the harmful effects of pesticides and herbicides, which contributed to water pollution and a reduction in soil fertility. Organic agriculture has recently been developed to reduce pollution, improve the quality of products, which replaces traditional methods with natural methods while safeguarding the environment.

Horticulture, however, is a sector of agriculture that consists of a set of agricultural and agronomic practices for the production of vegetables. It can be practiced as a hobby or as a professional activity. The crops - protected, semi-protected, and unprotected- can take place on earth or on another type of substrate, with a conventional method or with a biological and integrated method.

Substrate cultures, on the other hand, include different materials and types of cultivation, such as on natural substrates, synthetic substrates, and in a stream of water (it's called hydroponics).

Given the high management cost of substrate crops, this type of crop is mainly used for high-value flower and horticultural crops.

With the term horticulture, especially in the anthropological field, we can mean cultivation that does not require particular practices, nor the use of specific equipment, to differentiate it in the study of the methods of production from agriculture.

In modern metropolises, there are small but numerous and very important realities: vegetable gardens.

Urban horticulture wants to address these categories and communities as a means of aggregation and training to adopt a sustainable and self-sufficient social lifestyle.

Chapter 3.
VEGETABLE GARDENS IN HISTORY

Already in ancient Rome, two centuries before the birth of Christ, Marco Porcio Cato wrote the first practical manual of cultivation. Others followed him, perhaps discussing sowing and fertilizing in verse, like Virgil, or pretending to be in dialogue with an interlocutor interested in agricultural problems, like Marco Terenzio Varrone.

It is amazing that in such ancient times, men, lacking any possibility of scientifically checking what they did empirically in the fields, invented techniques that we still apply today almost without any modifications.

The ancients knew how to recognize the quality of the soil and how to correct it, and they knew the practice of rotations: 'the earth, changing its fruits, rests,' we read in the Georgics thirty years before Christ.

In 200 BC. Cato said: 'What is the first work to cultivate the land? Plow, and the second? Plow, and the third? Fertilize'.

Too bad that in those days, farmers too often allowed themselves to be misled by the strangest beliefs, blind to what they could see for themselves.

Alongside almost perfect technical standards on artichoke cultivation, one can, for example, find this advice: plant the seeds of varieties with thorns, each wrapped in a piece of a lettuce leaf, to harvest artichokes without thorns. One lesson, however, they soon learned and handed down to posterity: 'our inertia sterilizes the fields.'

The same Latin authors give us news of the cultivated vegetable plants; for example, the broad bean was considered a fundamental ingredient in the preparation of 'puls fabata', a term perhaps of Etruscan derivation which indicated polenta, or for the farratae (meals) mentioned by Juvenal and considered the traditional dish of the Etruscans. Peas, lentils, and chickpeas were also known and cultivated, so much so that the names of many Roman families are derived: Fabius from 'faba' (broad bean) or Cicero from 'cicer' (chickpea).

Other certainly cultivated vegetable species were garlic, onion, carrots, turnips, cabbage, and fennel, but also (already present in more remote times) lettuce and various shoots, such as celery and asparagus, coming from spontaneous plants.

According to ethnographers, the first step in developing primitive peoples, hunters, and gatherers of spontaneous products such as roots and shoots, was certainly horticulture, practiced particularly by women in those areas characterized by a hot-humid climate and on freed land from trees and woods employing fire.

The description of the various cultivation operations and the representation of the work are, however, detectable only in later periods, especially in the Roman one through specific murals and manuscripts also by authors from the colonies of the empire: classic is the 'De Re Rustica' by the Spanish Columella.

Chapter 4.
CHRONOLOGY OF VEGETABLES IN EUROPE

Now, let's see a detailed chronology of the diffusion of domesticated vegetables for the creation of the first private 'gardens'. Wild and spontaneous plants already known in the Mesolithic: celery, lettuce, asparagus, pea, onion, carrot, strawberry, raspberry, fig, cherry, plum, apple, honey, stone, vine, almond, olive.

From the Neolithic we know:

- Broad beans, headless cabbage, lentils, flax, turnips, garlic;
- With the Bronze Age began the cultivation of:
- Pea, chickpea, broad bean, lentil, fig, chestnut, walnut, olive.

In the Iron Age, we introduced: citron, almond, apple, pear, vine.

With the Greek colonization began a real explosion of new crops and relevant cultural innovations (think of the introduction of grafting for fruit trees):

- Cauliflower, broccoli, cabbage, watermelon, melon, celery, fennel, asparagus, pumpkin, chard, cucumber, strawberry, false bean, onion, garlic, carrot, peach, lemon, apricot, chestnut, walnut, pear, vine.

From the 14th century began the cultivation of spinach, aubergine, artichoke, bitter orange, new lemons, and citrons.

From the 16th century, the cultivation of various pumpkins, bell pepper, cauliflower, new artichokes, sweet orange.

From the 17th to the 19th century, there were contributions of new varieties and many cultural innovations involving many species, including tomato, pumpkin, pepper, celery, asparagus, strawberry, raspberry.

Finally, we recall:

- The introduction of the potato and sugar beet in the 18th century, the mandarin and persimmon in the 19th, and, finally, the grapefruit in the 20th century.
- Later, in Spain, invaded by the Arabs, Al Awam dedicates an entire book to agriculture in general, in which he summarizes the theories of all the ancient and contemporary scholars, applying them to more Mediterranean horticulture with particular references to soil needs, climate, and irrigation of vegetables.
- The plants described are always those we already know: it will be necessary to wait for the discovery of America (1492) to be able to increase the number of known and cultivated species, with the addition of tomatoes, peppers, potatoes, pumpkins and even beans (the cultivated by the Romans was Vigna unguiculata and not Phaseolus vulgaris).
- Botanical exchanges after the discovery of the new lands increased the cultivation of many new species destined for multiple uses: think that the tomato was initially imported as an ornamental plant and only many years later was it used, in Europe, for the consumption of the fruits.
- The evolution of agronomic science has then made it possible, through ever more refined selection practices, to obtain new and better cultivars or varieties of horticultural species.
- Particular shapes and dimensions and adaptability to different climatic and soil conditions have always been the guidelines of the research.
- New varieties selected for intensive cultivation in the open field, susceptible to mechanized harvesting, resistant to handling, and numerous diseases, which we can keep longer and longer, are only a part of the large list of vegetable essences on the market today.
- Even plants subject to particular treatments (just think of red chicory and white celery) that needed manipulation to achieve the characteristics for which they were known are grown today without problems and without resorting to post-harvest cultivation operations.
- Finally, new agronomic techniques, the use of means of protection, and knowledge of the different needs allow you to practice horticulture with pleasure and great satisfaction.

Chapter 5.
VEGETABLES OF AMERICA

When potatoes arrived from the New World, they were believed to be poisonous, so much so that the Bourbons of France had innovative potato dishes made to encourage their consumption. By 1840 it had become the primary source of livelihood for the peasant classes, especially in Ireland, and when the blight pandemic hit the island, the Irish moved en masse to the United States.

Potatoes are grown all over the world; they can be cooked in a thousand ways. Moreover, they are much caloric than any cereal and do not require complex cleaning operations. This makes them one of the essential plants for human nutrition: Any Weir knows it well, as the protagonist of the novel *The Man from Mar*s survives thanks to a diet of potatoes only!

On the other hand, when, between 1845 and 1849, due to the 'Great Famine,' the potato famine that struck Ireland, many people perished, and a large portion of Irish sailed to America, few, if any, knew that the land that welcomed them was the one from which the main source of food, the potato, had originated, reaching Europe only after the discovery of America, of the South, in this case, since the potato originally came from the Andes.

1492 was, in this sense - and also as regards the growing complexity of the ecological and environmental system and of the collateral and non-side effects of this complexity - a fundamental historical threshold that ushered in a 'new era,' in which the space of flows widened and intensified, in dimensional, qualitative, political, cultural, symbolic, biological terms, also due to the frequency and increase of movements, in an initially dilated time which in a short time gave life to a globalized and reticular planet.

From the beginning of the 19th century, the history of relations between the New and Old Worlds, which began at the end of the 15th century, underwent a consistent acceleration when 'migrations' became a macroscopic phenomenon, not only for plants, animals, and diseases but for the multitude of people from Europe, Asia, and Africa who moved (or were moved, as far as African Americans are concerned) to America.

The start and then the increase of the inter-exchanges between the two continents, previously separated by the ocean and unknown to each other, gave rise to a cognitive, geopolitical, but perhaps above all biological and environmental revolution, which had multiplier effects on the cultural, social, economic, ecological level.

In addition to the potato, beans, some varieties of pumpkins, cocoa, tobacco (and the virtues initially attributed to this plant), the large number of animals, microorganisms, or edible products, such as solanaceous plants including the tomato or maize, a grass domesticated in Mexico about 10,000 years ago, the biological migrations involved an enormous number of plants which, enriching the corpus of native species (on which the American botanical gardens conduct considerable research and a cataloging and conservation work), became part not only of the agricultural and urban or botanical landscape but of the US collections, herbariums, and botanical gardens.

The arrival of Europeans and Asians in both North and South America, however, not only generated a growing amount of contamination and hybridization but produced a very high level of erosion and cancellation of the autochthonous cultures, North American and South American lands, which were swept away, and with them was eroded, in addition to the real and perceived landscapes, the 'philosophy' and the symbolic system underlying that culture that had conceived that landscape and built that world.

To better understand the close interdependence between cultural and biological processes, it seems appropriate to underline that the American Indians, and the South Americans, were not decimated only due to opportunistic political choices and thanks to the planning of genocide; but, among others, also from pathogens against which the natives themselves were not immunized. In fact, they supported themselves with agriculture (they were 'gatherers') and hunting. The absence of breeding practices, on the other hand, widespread in Europe, had not allowed immunization against numerous zoonotic diseases that transmigrated from animals to humans, such as smallpox or tuberculosis.

In the "New World," the early people of Central America first developed corn, which they produced into hundreds of varieties that have now become a pin food and fodder crop around the world.

Tomatoes, potatoes, peppers, and beans are all western hemisphere crops that made their way back to Europe with Columbus and other explorers.

In South America, the Peruvians domesticated the potato, which now has now been bred into thousands of varieties of every imaginable size, shape, and color, and spread around the world as a staple calorie crop.

And in the land now called the US, early peoples planted what they called the Three Sisters, which consisted of squash, beans, and corn. These three vegetables are still grown together today because the beans provide nitrogen that the corn is hungry for, the corn provides the beans something to climb up, and the squash provides shade over the ground, which helps retain moisture. All three make excellent drying and storage crops for survival through long winters or when meat is scarce.

Columbus's ocean crossing had therefore triggered ambivalences, disadvantages, and advantages: in fact, in the exchange, both Europeans and Americans benefited from some of the botanical and zoological introductions after the discovery of America; on the other hand, by activating the dynamics of interaction between the continental systems, some pre-existing balances changed drastically.

An example regarding the 'community of plants' concerns the American forests, the intensive agriculture developed in America since the 16th century, and the world 'little glaciation' (which occurred between 1500 and the following 250 years), also attributable to the decline of the natives Americans, to the consequent reforestation (the natives created prairies through controlled fires, changing the composition of the forest systems), to the reduction of CO_2 emissions, and to the reduction of the greenhouse effect, with consequent lowering of world temperatures.

A further example is related to the presence of gardens, especially in the Mesoamerican area. While in Europe, the Hortus conclusus dominated - the garden of native flowers and plants, or the garden organized for therapeutic purposes, in which the plants were cataloged on the basis of medical principles; while, in the initial phase, the geometric scheme was in force, like the one adopted in Padua (Italy) (in 1545, in the oldest university garden in the world), later replaced by an 'English' layout and by schemes more closely adhering to the scientific ordering that to a specific geometry, i.e., the arrangements based on the 'Linnaean binomial system' - in specific and emblematic cases, in Mesomeric instead the culture of gardens had strong relationships with local resources, for example, water resources, and above all with the sense of the sacred.

When Cortez arrived in Mesomerica in 1519, he discovered, among others, the city of Tenochtitlan, today, Mexico City, where about 200,000 people lived. The populous city, like a fortress, was surrounded by a lake. For their food sustenance, the Aztecs had built chinampas, and floating gardens, transforming the marshes of Lake Texcoco into agricultural land. The floating gardens were rectangular and built on rafts made of woven wooden sticks. Mud was piled up on this floating base on which a layer of earth about a meter high was placed. The gardens were anchored thanks to the flexible fronds of some weeping willows; they had a network of canals around them to allow the passage of canoes, making up a network of about 9,000 ha. They were planted with corn, beans, pumpkins, tomatoes, peppers, and flowers, also including species with recognized therapeutic virtues in a geographical area where medical science based on phytotherapy had already had a great development, giving life to an analog of the botanical garden, which was conceived by the Medical School of Salerno.

In the sources, it is reported that the Aztec gardens produced seven crops a year, but Cortez, who was interested only in plundering the cashable riches of the Aztec civilizations and, in their dominion, ordered their destruction. The North American myth of the 'Great American wilderness,' then, does not restore the entire and complex fabric relating to the relationship between man and nature in America (North and South). A relationship that concerns both the culture of the North American natives and that of the pre-Columbian civilizations, and however reveals the different effect of urban settlements on the environment and the unequal relationship of the settled populations with the territory. Above all, if seen in comparative terms with the European one, where a space dominated by the simultaneous presence of 'ager' and 'urbs' (agro and material city), extensive agriculture, mammoth and permanent cathedrals, and stone cities. Environments which, even more, if looked at comparatively, could be understood as a mirror of the local reality and as an expression of the feedback between the co-evolutionary biological structure and the cultural transformation.

It was largely the post-Colombian phase and the arrival of the Europeans that triggered a macro-environmental and cultural metamorphosis, but it was not the only action of the 'subjects' that changed the conditions of the American continent, as much as the enormous amount of contributing causes and among they are bio-cultural contingencies interpreted as significant interacting elements in a complex system.

Therefore, the close connection between culture and biology should be noted, and it is also through this link that it becomes interesting to explore the evolution of gardens, the botanical discipline, and the birth of the Botanical Gardens in America, places where science, culture, economy and productivity, conservation, biology, society, work together.

Chapter 6.
FROM THE PILGRIMS
TO THE VICTORY PIONEERS

During the time of the Pilgrims, everybody was a gardener: a full-time job to make sure to survive healthily and in abundance. Peas, barley, and corn were the primary staple crops, but they also grew onions, carrots, and other vegetables grew from seeds they brought from England.

Vegetable gardening was not an optional activity at the time but was necessary for the livelihood of the community. For this reason, every one learned this art, at least until they became wealthy enough to force slaves to do it for them.

Slaves were implied in all aspects of farming and gardening, from planting to irrigating and harvesting tobacco and cotton. Also, the slaves maintained their own vegetable gardens and raised chickens.

As people expanded into new territories, Pilgrims took their seeds and started vegetable gardens wherever they stopped and settled.

Thomas Jefferson, for example, was one of the first famous gardeners. It was his passion, and he was also involved in collecting various vegetables from all over the world, testing them, and also saving the seeds. He was so painstaking that he even kept records of his own gardening experiments.

Then came a period of greater prosperity, with agriculture experiencing more methods of growing vegetables and food in a more automated and faster way. An aspect that shattered under the blows of the Second World War, a moment in which vegetable gardeners became essential. Growing your own food was a matter of life and death since food rationing was severe.

After the war, there was a return to mass agriculture, with the use of chemical herbicides which in the long run led to the degradation of the land.

At that point - and we are not that far away from today in terms of time - we are witnessing a return of vegetable gardening as an option also for the survival of the planet.

This revival is organic, pure, pristine, and local. A renewed interest on the part of many people in creating a rich, sustainable, healthy, and zero-kilometer personal garden to also enrich the local community.

In America, they call them 'victory gardens' and are considered patriotic. Emblematic in this regard is the initiative of the then First Lady Michelle Obama, who, in the middle of the White House, planted a vegetable and organic garden.

And here we come: if you are here, it is because you have learned the lesson of history and of the best Pilgrims: build your own garden of victory.

To support your health, well-being, and our beautiful planet at the same time!

Chapter 7.
LEARN FROM THE PAST TO IMPROVE THE FUTURE

Cultivating a vegetable garden personally is becoming a real trend, and those who do not have their own land often look for alternative solutions ranging from cultivation on the balcony to putting themselves on the list for a vegetable garden made available by the Municipality. Now there are even hanging greenhouses that can be anchored to the buildings, creating a green space of 2 square meters by making a prior authorization request to the condominium assembly.

However, in this collection of books, we will take care of building our vegetable garden by being able to count on a large and adequate space to grow your own personal vegetable garden.

After all, there are many reasons why each of us should try to have our own garden:

it allows us to get closer to nature and its rhythms, much more in line with those of the well-being of the person than those that modern life imposes on us;

it takes us away from the stress of routine, allowing us to unwind from the problems that afflict us in everyday life;

it makes us aware of the importance and satisfaction that comes from seeing something sprout and grow from a simple seed;

it gives us the possibility of having quality food, tasty, healthy, and much cheaper than that of the supermarket;

it allows us to cultivate rare native and non-native species that are disappearing because they are not very profitable for industrial cultivation (as preppers and seed savers do all over the world).

Well, in the next books, we will find out together what the creation of a vegetable garden consists of and how to best carry it forward!

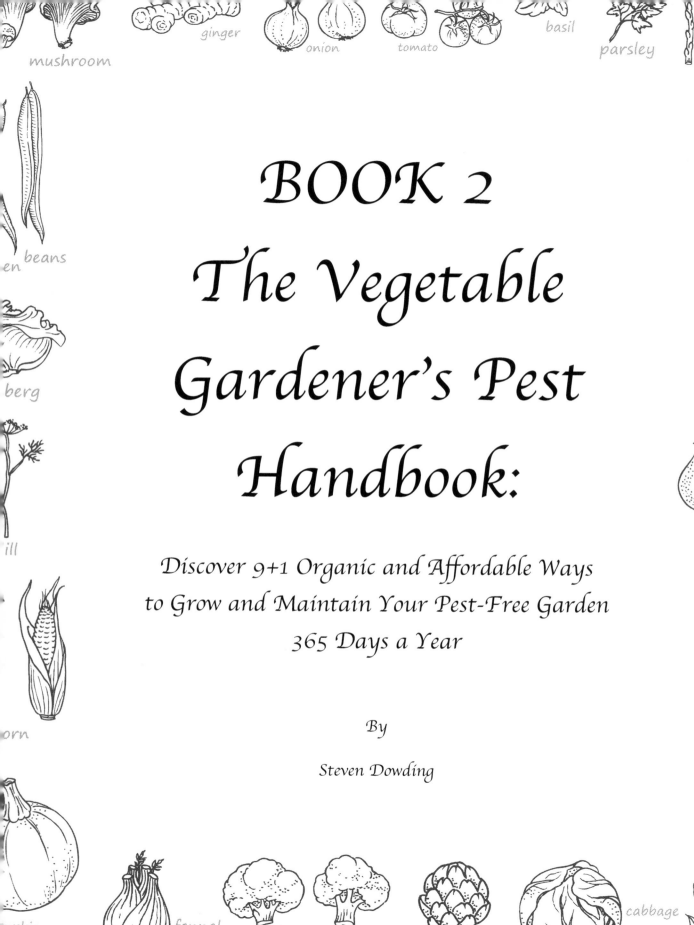

BOOK 2
The Vegetable Gardener's Pest Handbook:

Discover 9+1 Organic and Affordable Ways
to Grow and Maintain Your Pest-Free Garden
365 Days a Year

By

Steven Dowding

Chapter 1.
A PEST FREE GARDEN 365 DAYS A YEAR

Everyone would like to eat healthy, beautiful, and tasty vegetables produced with respect for the environment and minimizing the use of synthetic chemicals. For this reason, for years, there has been a continuous growth of the so-called organic agriculture, where the production method places many limits on the use of pesticides.

Yet when we buy an apple from organic farming, it appears red, juicy, and crunchy: how is it possible to obtain beautiful and good products without using traditional defense products? How to keep insects away without using insecticide? How to combat fungi without immediately applying a fungicide?

The Basics of Organic Farming

To understand how this kind of 'magic' that casts so many shadows on the world of organic agriculture is possible, I'm forced to take the topic a little off the bat... but I'll try to be concise!

Organic farming aims to grow vegetables, fruit, and arable land in complete soil rich in all fertility factors. In this sense, chemical fertility is put into the background and not pushed to the highest level. On the contrary, great care is taken to maintain physical and microbiological fertility, aspects that the conventional farmer a little too neglects. In other words, organic agriculture seeks to create an environment that is as suitable as possible for the development of plants without forcing them.

Furthermore, the plants are grown within a complex agroecosystem, far from the ecological simplification that accompanies conventional farms. The fight against weeds is not so exasperated and, therefore, on the sides of the fields - and a little even in the middle of the crops - there are numerous plants which, although 'unwanted,' help to make the ecosystem more stable. For example, within this spontaneous vegetation, many useful insects can find refuge – and therefore multiply – such as some predators of annoying plant parasites.

The Right Plant in the Right Place

One of the first steps to reduce the possibility of diseases developing in our garden is to choose the most suitable plants – and varieties – for it. Each vegetable has its specific characteristics in terms of water and thermal needs. Suppose we can meet the needs in terms of water through careful irrigation. In that case, we cannot do the same to satisfy the needs of temperature, a fundamental factor to guarantee the plants the ideal conditions to carry out all the biochemical and physiological processes (photosynthesis, respiration, etc. essential for obtaining good fruit. In more detail, we should remember that each species has its optimal growth temperature and well-defined critical and cardinal temperatures. The latter is the minimum and maximum temperatures below and above which the vital functions stop and then resume when the temperature returns to optimal. Critical temperatures, on the other hand, are those above and below which irreparable damage does not allow anything to be produced.

In other words, therefore, if we live in the mountains and only have a small shaded space at the back of the house, it is useless to try to grow tomatoes. If we persist in doing so, we must be aware that the production will not be the same as we could get in the most suitable areas. Furthermore, plants will probably be more prone to attack by pathogens.

If, on the other hand, we choose the right plant in the right place, the probability that the plant will fall ill due to fungi or bacteria or be affected by parasites is much lower because it will be much more 'at ease'. A bit as if we were forced to go to the tropics with a ski suit or to the poles in a swimsuit: a little dehydration or a cold is the least we could expect!

Lay the Table for Our Vegetables

It's not a typo: before setting our table with grown vegetables, we need to worry about setting theirs so that they grow in full health. Let's think: is enjoying a delicious Sunday lunch the same as swallowing a few pills containing all the nutrients our body needs? I would say not. For plants, roughly the same is true: this is why they react better in well-structured soil, with a good supply of nutrients and drainage. Providing them with micro and macro elements of fertility is not enough if they find themselves living in sterile soil.

To have healthy plants without running immediately to pesticides, we must ensure that the plants have soil free from stagnation (who would like to live with their feet constantly in the water?). This factor predisposes to the onset of many fungal diseases.

A good supply of organic matter is essential: once, there was a lot of it in the fields (animal husbandry was present in many farms and manure was the order of the day); today, the soils are a bit poor in this important factor of fertility. Too much weight has been given to chemical fertility (chemical fertilizers), and now we find ourselves with very low levels of organic matter because our soils are so poorly structured that plants struggle to deepen their root system. In our gardens, we must avoid repeating the mistake and incorporate a good dose of compost (perhaps self-produced) every year. The idea is to place it sometime before planting so that the compost can begin the slow mineralization phase and release the nutrients into the soil.

The planting distance is also important: the distance on the row and between the rows must be adjusted to allow the plants to develop sufficiently and without competing with each other. Competition means stress: we know how much this affects our immune defenses! When we go through a period of intense work and have a thousand things on our minds, it is easier for small or big problems to arise for our health. The same goes for garden plants

The Importance of Irrigation

Irrigation plays a primary role in the spread of plant diseases. Firstly because pathogens are comfortable in humid contexts, for this reason, it is important to avoid the presence of water on the leaves, which, as far as possible, should always be dry. It is, therefore, better to abandon the classic water hose and resort to irrigation 'from below or by flowing or, even better, using micro-sprinklers or dripping lines, which, among other things, can facilitate interventions as we can easily combine them with a time programmer. But be careful: directly irrigating the soil does not solve all the problems! There are also numerous diseases affecting the root system, and also, in this case, they are favored by stagnant humidity.

The advice is to resort to abundant but well-spaced irrigations, avoiding wetting every day. In this way, the quantity of free water is reduced, and, generally, the development of pathogens is made more difficult. But this practice has another advantage: rinsing after a few days, the most superficial layer of soil dries up, pushing the vegetables to deepen their root system. A deep and well-developed root system explores a greater amount of soil, absorbs more nutrients, and can better resist any water shocks. In fact, what would happen if we accustomed our plants to being watered every day, and then, just as we were away for a weekend, a heat wave should arrive? A superficial root system would not know where to get the necessary water, and the plants would enter a situation of great stress.

Furthermore, irrigation - also, in this case, in the dock, there is, above all, sprinkler irrigation - can favor the ascent of pathogens from the soil (where they often overwinter) to the leaves of plants. The impact of water droplets on the ground, like natural rain, raises small soil particles capable of carrying the mushroom propagules on the plant.

Now that we have learned the basics for building a pesticide-free garden, let's discover together the main and surprising natural methods to do it!

Straight to the point, we don't have a second to lose against parasites! :)

Chapter 2.
FIRST THING FIRST: PREVENTION

From plants found spontaneously in nature, it is possible to obtain excellent liquid products to be used in the garden to prevent some parasitic adversities. The production and use of plant extracts, macerations, and decoctions have long been used in organic farming with proven beneficial effects for crops.

Cultivating with an environmentally friendly method means, above all, avoiding the use of many chemical products for fertilization and defense against diseases and parasites and a preference for substances of natural and biodegradable origin.

Macerates and plant extracts are certainly among the most effective, simple, and economical solutions and are of great help in cultivation as they perform several exciting functions.

In the organic garden, it is necessary to ensure that the plants are able to be strong and resilient and that they are able to withstand any pathogenic or parasitic attacks thanks to their own defense mechanisms, which the macerates help to strengthen.

In organic cultivation, it becomes imperative to focus on prevention to reduce the likelihood of particularly intense attacks by harmful insects or fungal diseases. The products we can then use to eradicate these adversities have less strong effects than conventional ones, and we cannot expect the same knockdown power and persistence. Consequently, it becomes useful to focus on removing the causes that can trigger serious damage, starting from the assumption that it is not possible to eliminate them entirely but rather to bring them below an acceptable threshold.

What Are Macerates

Macerates are liquid products that are obtained by soaking harvested plants. The substances contained inside impregnate the water and enrich it with useful elements, constituting an excellent natural do-it-yourself defense in the organic garden. Some macerated extracts, which we will see later in detail, are more suitable for preventing diseases or parasitic attacks on vegetables. Others, on the other hand, have a fertilizing effect and can be used to create a sort of 'fertigation,' i.e., irrigation with water rich in plant nutrients. Furthermore, we should note that macerates with preventive action against diseases and insects can also be used on many ornamental plants and fruit trees, one more reason to try to make them.

Advantages and Disadvantages of Macerates

The extracts that aim to prevent diseases and harmful insects make it possible to reduce or eliminate treatments with products that, although environmentally friendly, in some cases still have an environmental impact, such as copper.

The disadvantage of wanting to look for one is that of the time and effort required for research, identification, and collection of suitable plants, for the preparation of the macerates in all the necessary steps, and distribution.

Another aspect to bear in mind is that we cannot store the macerated products for long and therefore they must be prepared every time and used as soon as possible, once they are ready.

However, once you master the process, it becomes much easier to practice over time and will take less time. So let's see which are the most common plants for the preparation of macerates.

Preparation of macerates: which plants to use?

In nature, it is possible to find many plants to be used to prepare macerates, but it can be helpful to know where they grow the most, how to recognize them, and how to collect them.

Before taking action, however, make sure you know the importance of prevention in organic gardens and the advantages of do-it-yourself macerates.

Nettle

Nettle is one of the best-known and most used plants for the preparation of macerates. We can easily find it in uncultivated areas along ditches and wetlands from spring until all summer. There are two species of nettle: Urtica dioica and Urtica urens; they are kind of similar to each other but not to be confused with the false nettle, which is the Lamium, a plant that can be recognized when it flowers by its small white or pink flowers, which the nettle does not have. The short nettle macerate repels aphids thanks to its content of stinging substances, including acetylcholine, serotonin, formic acid, and histamine.

Horsetail

Horsetail (Equisetum arvense) is a herbaceous species characterized by green stems and a little rough to the touch, with leaves arranged in a sunburst pattern. It is not a plant found everywhere like other species; you have to look for it with a pinch of patience. It is located along ditches, in escarpments, and in humid environments, generally from late spring until all summer. The feature that makes it excellent for the preparation of macerates is its silicon content, an element that helps plants resist fungal diseases.

Garlic

For decoctions or macerated garlic preparation, it is outstanding to use the garlic you buy for cooking. However, if it were available in the garden, we could collect some plants and use them whole for this purpose, even if the stems were still green. Garlic contains allicin and is used for its fungicidal properties, but it also has insect-repellent properties.

Onion

In this case, it is also possible to use purchased onions, but if present in the garden, all the better. Onions are rich in sulfur-based compounds that exhibit antibiotic properties.

Male fern

The ferns are found above all in the undergrowth up to about 1700 m of altitude, and the leaves are collected for the preparation of the macerates. The fern contains phyllite, a substance with an antiparasitic effect.

Tomato

Even the leaves of tomato plants have an excellent effect if used to prepare macerates. In addition to the actual leaves, the females are also perfect, i.e., the axillary shoots that must be regularly eliminated from these plants to ensure their single-stemmed growth. The collection of tomato leaves and females can therefore take place throughout the summer.

The stem and leaves of the tomato are covered in hairs that give off a typical smell when rubbed. They contain solanine, a toxic alkaloid that constitutes a form of defense for the plant itself against animal and fungal parasites. We can exploit this property for the preparation of macerates.

Now that you've gathered all the plants, it's time to get ready.

Chapter 3.
DIY MACERATES STRATEGIES

Preparing do-it-yourself macerates for the defense of the organic garden, to keep parasites away and prevent diseases, is not particularly complicated. Before proceeding with the preparation, however, make sure you know the importance of prevention in the organic garden and the advantages of do-it-yourself plant macerates;

have picked the right plants. Precisely what we learned in the first 2 Chapters!

1. Nettle

For nettle harvesting, as a precaution, it is essential to wear thick gloves since the plant stings due to its content of substances such as acetylcholine, serotonin, histamine, and formic acid. For harvesting, it is advisable to use a bucket and scissors or a knife to cut the stems. In fact, it is not necessary to uproot the plants because the roots are not used to prepare the macerates. Cutting only the stems avoids eliminating the plants, which will thus grow back and will be helpful for future research.

The plant is quite voluminous and light: you need a lot to reach 1 kg. The proportions for soaking are 1 kg of plant in 10 liters of water.

With nettle, you can make extracts with a deterrent action to ward off parasites that affect practically all vegetables and partly also against red spider mites and bedbugs. Let's see how to proceed.

Extract

The nettle extract is a short maceration in which the plants remain soaked for a day or two at the most. After this time, the formic acid contained in the nettle is still present and can be used precisely to remove the parasites from the attacked plants. Or even towards those who are still healthy, for disease prevention. In this case, the extract must not be diluted but sprayed as it is on the plants, given that the short maceration time did not make it very concentrated. Before the treatment, accurate filtering is essential, regardless of the tool you intend to use for spraying, whether a pump or a small vaporizer. We can use colanders or even non-woven fabric, which is usually used in the garden to protect vegetables from the cold.

The extracts are distributed directly on the plants, from vegetable, fruit, and even ornamental plants, wetting them uniformly to guarantee a good coverage of the whole crop.

The foliar treatments with these extracts and macerations are the only cases in which the aerial parts of the crops are wet and typically left dry so as not to favor fungal pathologies.

Let's not forget that nettle macerate is also excellent for fertilizing and, therefore, can act as a biological fertilizer.

2. Horsetail

Macerated

For a 10-liter container of water, 400 grams of horsetail or a similar proportion are enough, to be left to macerate for a week, as in the case of nettle, a few grams of rock flour, algae, or bentonite added to the liquid help to reduce the bad smells emanating from fermentation. After a week, it is possible to use the macerate after careful filtering and 1:5 dilution. In biodynamic agriculture, horsetail decoction is also widely used, which is obtained by boiling the plants for 40-60 minutes.

The horsetail macerate, sprayed on the aerial parts of all plants, helps strengthen them thanks to its high silicon content, making plant cells more resistant. In this way, the plants are subjected to fewer attacks by fungal pathogens, making it possible to reduce cupric treatments.

3. Garlic

For garlic-based preparations, it is better to proceed hot, by boiling or infusion, because, with cooking, its repellent effect against insects is maximized due to the strong smell.

In particular, it is useful in removing parasites, including aphids, bedbugs, and white cabbage, nocturnal moths (various species of moths that attack in particular at night), and attic. Considering that, among all these, bed bugs, in particular, are tough insects to fight, even with the insecticides available, it is advisable to regularly try the use of this macerate.

Decoction

Three hundred grams of garlic, bulbs, or even part of the stem, must be boiled in 10 liters of water. If you didn't have a large pot of this size, you could still obtain the necessary proportions (150 grams in 5 liters). After which, it is left to cool, filtered, and sprayed on the plants.

Infusion

The preparation of the infusion is more convenient because it requires a lower quantity of water to heat than the decoction. In this case, it is a question of pouring a liter of boiling water over 300-400 grams of fresh garlic and leaving it to infuse for about a quarter of an hour. Once the infusion has cooled, it must be filtered, diluted in 10 liters of cold water, and sprayed on the plants to be protected.

4. Onion

Decoction

The onion decoction or macerate helps keep away parasites and other harmful insects such as bed bugs or the carrot fly. This macerate can also be helpful for dipping the roots of vegetable seedlings before transplanting. In this way, they will be more resistant to the attacks of certain harmful terrestrial insects.

To prepare the onion decoction, just boil about 100 grams of the bulb; better if the ground is in 5 liters of water for a quarter of an hour. Then leave to cool and spray on the plants after filtration.

Macerated

In this case, 100 grams of onion must be cold macerated for a week in 2 liters of water to use the filtered and diluted product.

We can also use garlic and onion together in a more powerful mixed macerate.

5. Male Fern

We suggest a thrifty collection of its leaves to not impact too much on the ecosystem in which ferns are found. For example, prepare a small macerate in which 300 grams of ferns are soaked in 3 liters of water for a week. After this time, it is diluted 1:10 as usual, filtered, and the preparation is used for foliar treatments against scale insects of fruit and ornamental plants and to keep slugs and slugs away from the garden.

6. Tomato

Macerated

The preparation of this macerate is much shorter than the previous ones. Just collect about a pound of leaves and females, and chop them with scissors or a knife, so that the internal liquid comes out easily. Subsequently, immerse it in 1 liter of water for a few hours, from a minimum of 2 to a maximum of 5. After this, there is no need for dilution but certainly scrupulous filtering as in the previous cases.

The product is used on cabbages or other Brassicaceae for their protection from white cabbage and altic. The cabbage lady is a butterfly whose larva feeds itself on the leaves of the cabbages, in some cases leaving only the ribs intact. At the same time, the altics are responsible for those numerous small holes that are often found on rocket leaves, radishes, and some cabbages.

During the summer, the autumn cabbages are transplanted, and the tomatoes are present in the garden, so the preparation of this macerate is certainly easy to make.

Chapter 4.
ORGANIC DEFENSE STRATEGIES

The biological defense of a garden focuses entirely on prevention. That is, implementing the appropriate agronomic techniques (such as using nets and mulching) and exploiting all the biological solutions designed to create the conditions so that colonies of parasites or fungal spores do not develop. Not wanting to use synthetic products with strong knockdown power to defend a vegetable garden, we must work above all on prevention.

A cornerstone of this preventive approach involves the use of stimulating and enhancers of the natural defenses of plants. Therefore products of natural origin (rocks, other plants, etc.) are to be used preventively and not only when insects or fungi appear.

The main advantage of organic preparations is the possibility of using them at any moment of vegetative development, both in the vegetable garden and in the orchard, since they have no shortage times.

Let's start from the premise that plants grown correctly (temperature, irrigation, sun, etc.) are less subject to attacks by parasites and fungi. Plants suffer from two leading causes: biotic stress (attacks by fungal diseases, insects, bacteria, etc.) and/or abiotic (suffering related to factors of temperature, humidity, light, water, etc.). Plants weakened by abiotic stress will be more fragile to attacks by fungi and insects. In particular, fertilization is significant, and you can learn more about this topic in this Chapter.

Instead, let's see what arrows we have to our bow to defend plants from fungi and parasites. A biological defense strategy must consider the entire life span of insects: eggs, larvae, and adults because each requires different approaches.

1. Physioactivators

Physioactivators are the last frontier and arise from various solutions that have already found positive results in agriculture. A 'bomb' of energy obtained from the mix of valuable substances, all-natural, with a high concentration of fulvic, humic, humine, macro, and microelements. The result is that it allows maximum assimilation of the nutrients present in the soil, stimulates the early and vigorous development of roots, and revitalizes degraded or dull soils.

They can be used both on the roots and the leaves: the foliar treatment is carried out from April to July, while the foliar treatment is in February, March, August, and September.

2. Traps

These are small yellow adhesive sheets that attract the adults of many species of flying insects, such as aphids and ground gnats. They play a dual role: they are a 'sentinel' ready to signal the presence of parasites at the first appearance and partly allow the massive capture of insects by limiting their further reproduction. To prevent infestation, it is important that traps are set early in the season before pest populations begin to reproduce.

3. Dusts

Against fungal diseases, we can use powders that prevent the establishment of spores and tend to reduce environmental humidity. The rock dust performs a dehydrating action, discouraging the presence of snails, slugs, and fungal diseases. Sprayed on crops, it creates a physical barrier on the foliage and an unfavorable environment for developing fungi and insects.

Kaolin for example is a white mineral and creates a homogeneous film of milky color on plants, with strong adhesive power. In addition to creating and reducing humidity and avoiding fungal diseases, the material is unsuitable for oviposition and dissuades the insects from settling on the leaves. Furthermore, the white color reflects the sun's rays, protecting the plant from sunburn.

Zeolite has the natural ability to quickly absorb the humidity present in the environment, allowing it to prevent and strongly limit the development and diffusion of cryptogams. It performs two actions: it subtracts the water necessary for the germination of the spores and stimulates a rapid healing of the micro-wounds, one of the main ways for the fungi to penetrate inside the plant.

Sodium hydrogen carbonate is a white crystalline powder that creates an unfavorable environment for the proliferation of spores and protects plants from the attack of Oidium and Ticchiolattura. It acts by contact, raising the pH on the leaf surface, collapsing the fungal cell walls, and dehydrating the spores. Because of these multiple modes of action, sodium hydroxycarbonate has a low potential to favor the onset of resistance.

Against fungal diseases (mal white, scab, downy mildew, rust, etc.), we remind you that we can also use sulfur and copper-based fungicides, permitted in organic farming.

4. BONUS: Natural 'Allies'

As we already pointed out, Nature offers us a range of valuable solutions to create the conditions so that insects do not lay their eggs and to ward off parasites already present. Obviously, in the case of extensive infestations, only crop protection products can ensure effective results. But we have many tools to prevent the problem: let's get to know them!

The nettle extract has energetic properties, contained in the cellular juices of the nettle, easily assimilated by plants that need to overcome periods of greater energy consumption due to biotic and abiotic stress. It helps control the development of parasites such as Mites, Aphids, Altice, Carpocapse, Moths, Alternaria (black spots), and Moniliosi and stimulates plant growth.

Propolis helps fight damage caused by biotic and abiotic stress. It enhances the defenses of plants against fungal and bacterial attacks and has a healing action in wounds caused by trauma, pruning, or hailstorms.

Another vital ally is Neem seeds which contain an active ingredient (azadirachtin) that carries out a phagorepellent action: the insects are disgusted and move away. In particular, it is repellent for defoliating insects (Psylla, Doriphora, Nocturnal, or Thrips) but without influencing the action of bees and pollinators.

In case of the first parasites, we can use rapeseed oil: an effective insecticide against many species of insects, such as aphids, scale insects, red spider mites, and whiteflies, which infest the plants in the garden. It forms a film that covers the insect, killing it by asphyxiation. It is effective in all stages of insect development: eggs, larvae, and adults.

Aphids and scale insects produce a sticky honeydew that smears the plants and generates fungal diseases such as sooty mold: soft soap is handy on these occasions. Wash the honeydew and soot from the leaves and create an environment that is not suitable for their development.

Finally, against slugs and snails, we can create a 'natural barrier' using products based on clay granules which develop an impassable dry area for these animals, as they would dehydrate. Simply distribute the granules around the plants to be protected to build an off-limits area for slugs and snails. It does not contain any dangerous substances and is therefore safe for domestic or wild animals, such as birds and hedgehogs, which are natural enemies of snails.

Chapter 5.
GARDENER'S PEST HANDBOOK HACKS

The use of macerated vegetables in the garden is undoubtedly related to the availability of the plants with which to prepare them. However, their constant preparation is possible by identifying the areas where these grow and are available for regular harvesting.

In fact, occasional spraying of the macerates cannot have a decisive effect. Instead, it is their constancy that makes them excellent allies in the protection of organic gardens.

Ideally, we should prepare and distribute these macerates weekly or every two weeks. For some insects, we can choose from more than one of these (for example, against aphids); for others, a more specific plant is needed, as in the case of the male fern, for the removal of scale insects.

To conclude, we can see how and when it is convenient to treat vegetables with the macerates mentioned above:

Most of the above macerates can be used during all stages of crop development. With the exception, however, of the garlic infusion and decoction, which must not be used for the 15 days preceding the harvest in order not to penalize the organoleptic qualities of the vegetables themselves;

As for the best moments for distributing the macerates, as for any other treatment, it is essential to choose the coolest hours of the day. In fact, it must be considered that with the treatments, water is distributed on the aerial part of the plants and that with the direct sun of the central hours of the day, burns to the vegetation could occur;

We should always consider that using macerates in the garden is for preventive purposes, as already expressed above. While in the case of attacks by harmful insects or fungal pathologies in progress, we should still resort to products with an actual insecticide or fungicide action. Paying attention to choosing those allowed in organic farming that has a reduced environmental impact compared to conventional ones.

Macerates and compost: macerates can also irrigate the compost pile, especially in dry periods when composting require higher humidity. Otherwise, the process of decomposition of all waste slows down. In this regard, it is helpful to know how to make compost and distribute it in the ground.

macerates and Personal Protective Equipment: the use of the macerates and their distribution does not require the use of classic Personal Protective Equipment, which we must rigorously wear during treatments with cupric products and with other products that provide for it and for which it is always necessary to consult the 'label. In the case of macerated products, what is distributed is a liquid that derives from the maceration of plants without adding any substance that can irritate them.

Finally, we should emphasize that the macerates are biodegradable products, which leave no environmental pollution.

Chapter 6.
SMALL PHARMACY
FOR THE ORGANIC GARDEN

What if all the previous precautions are not always sufficient to combat parasites and pathogens that can affect our vegetables? When the choice of crops and agronomic attention is not completely effective, we have to resort to pesticides that are as environmentally friendly as possible.

Obviously, these preparations - usually of natural origin - are less effective than the corresponding synthetic products and, therefore, it is important to go into the garden often to check the state of the crops, carefully evaluate the phytosanitary and development conditions so as to intervene without as soon as the first warning signs appear.

Marseille soap can also be a valid ally: dissolved in 10-20 grams per liter of water, the preparation has a good insecticide action and acts quickly, especially against aphids. Better to use it in the coolest hours of the day because it can cause foliar burns to the most sensitive varieties.

Other useful preparations for the containment of parasites - but which we cannot prepare independently - are the products based on Bacillus thuringiensis and those based on pyrethrum.

Furthermore, do not forget the products based on iron orthophosphate for the control of slugs and snails if their 'invasion' is such as to suggest their containment.

For products based on copper, sulfur, and the like - even if allowed in organic farming - we must contact a specialized retailer. But if we are careful and scrupulously follow good agronomic practices, the purchase of plant protection products will be truly reduced to a minimum!

BOOK 3
Vegetable Gardening
Hacks:

Vertical, Balcony, Shady, Container,
Small-Scale, Raised Bed, Veggie,
No-Dig Hydroponic Vegetable Gardening,
High Yielding Wall, Wide Rows, Deep Soil,
Companion Planting

By

Steven Dowding

Chapter 1.
A MATTER OF CHOICE

For thousands of years, man has collected and selected many plants to be used for his own diet and has reared them in a wise way, obtaining, over time, plants with ever better quality characteristics.

The success of a vegetable garden is influenced by some parameters that are fundamental for the growth of healthy plants that give genuine and tasty products:

- Sun exposure: direct sunlight provides the best results;
- Irrigation: regular water supply is an essential prerogative for optimal growth;
- Soil: if possible, it must be flat, of medium texture, fresh and fertile;
- Defense against adversity: it is the best way to obtain a favorable production;
- Choice of plants: based on the place and time of year where you are.
- Taken together, these factors form the foundations of an agroecosystem where man is the central pivot that articulates the entire functioning mechanism: YOU will make the difference.

It takes little to have a rich vegetable garden that produces delicious products; simply follow my following instructions on how to grow vegetables and achieve excellent results.

In addition, there are many techniques for cultivating the land and creating a perfect vegetable garden for your needs.

In the following chapters, therefore, we will discover the best-known techniques one by one.

Chapter 2.
VERTICAL VEGETABLE GARDENING

The pioneer of this type of gardening was Patrick Blanc, a Parisian scholar, and botanist who covered facades and public and private areas of the French capital and beyond with his spectacular green installations.

He set up the first green wall at the La Villette museum in Paris.

Gradually, other green architects have sprung up who have indulged themselves worldwide with ever more refined green walls.

From Hotel Athenaeum in London to Madrid (Caixa Forum), from New Delhi (French Embassy) to Bangkok (Emporium Shopping Mall), via Taipei (Concert Hall) and Milan (Bosco Verticale). And just to cite the best-known examples.

How to Make a Vertical Vegetable Garden

These are harmonious compositions of plants created on stratified modules or panels (PVC and felt) put in a metal cage. This cage is then fixed to the vertical walls (internal vertical gardens) or the walls (external vertical gardens). Moreover, it can also be self-supporting (supported by special structures).

It is a hydroponic garden in which irrigation is made up of a mix of rainwater and fertilizers and is constant. And it is conducted using a drip system that starts from the top of the wall. So the soil is not needed.

There are different kinds of green walls, all adaptable to any architectural modular and surface, according to specific needs:

- partial or total cladding of external facades;
- retaining walls;
- self-supporting walls;
- fences.

Vertical Garden on Wall

Gardens are generally fractured to cover walls using large panels or assemblable modules. These integrate with the features of the wall to ensure the functionality of doors and windows.

Contemporary systems specific for the creation of vertical gardens find greater application in two types of systems:

Ventilated facade, crucial for covering the external walls of large buildings

Sound-absorbing walls, designed exclusively to guarantee acoustic insulation and beautify urban areas near railway yards, road and motorway junctions, and railways.

The panels practically constitute the inorganic substrate for the vegetation with which they are covered and allow it to grow by exploiting the hydroponic cultivation technique, i.e., without using soil.

They are fully equipped with automated micro-irrigation systems that drip fertilizer-enriched water. And thus make maintenance undemanding.

Furthermore, they are normally positioned a couple of centimeters from the wall to allow air circulation and avoid stagnation of humidity.

Vertical Garden on Ventilated Facade

Among the most widespread systems in vertical greenery, it involves a construction technique for assembling the panels already integrated with vegetation. That has the undoubted advantage of guaranteeing the replaceability even of a single panel.

Approximately 12 months is the period for the plants to settle from the installation of the system. Generally, the cultural substrates to support the vegetation (generally with plants selected by nurserymen) guarantee uniform water distribution and a green surface throughout the year.

The panels are generally made of oxidized aluminum sheets with a cell structure to house grooves and plants designed to facilitate the water flow.

Moreover, the back side of the panels is blind, so there is no possibility of humidity for the walls of the building. Furthermore, the modules are installed to the wall with an aluminum grid that acts as a support, resistant to atmospheric agents and humidity.

An air chamber is left between the façade and the internal wall of the building to guarantee ventilation and thermo-acoustic insulation.

Then, the plants are placed on a polypropylene irrigating sub-layer, which encloses a core of peat and expanded perlite, i.e., a volcanic rock that retains humidity, recreating the natural habitat for plant growth, a very widespread technique in hydroponic crops.

Vertical Garden on Sound-Absorbing Barriers

They are self-supporting barriers, single or double-sided, especially suitable for decreasing noise and improving urban aesthetics near motorways or railway stations.

Steel uprights support the structure on which the panels are already welded to the metal mesh. Very light substrates are used for filling, which can retain water in the best possible way and supply the necessary nutrients to all grafted plants.

Vertical Garden Plants

It is fundamental to choose the species carefully to be planted, with respect to the specificity of the native flora and also the climate.

The choice almost always goes to low-maintenance varieties, which ask for little care and interventions during the year.

Another crucial feature is that they must be ground cover and have space for climbing plants, pergola plants, bushes, shrubs, and hanging plants.

Very light varieties are usually preferred, especially those whose roots do not need to sink into the too-deep soil (30 kg per square meter). Otherwise, the risk compromises the integrity of walls and buildings.

The choice of essences, however, must take into account several factors:

- the area in which the building is located geographically (exposure to the sun, windiness, orientation...);
- water requirement;
- flowering;
- the type of plant and substrate used.

The vegetation must be laid in favorable climatic and environmental conditions: it will be vital to monitoring its adaptation and development, especially in the first 8-12 months after laying.

Variety of Plants for the Vertical Garden

The most used are the microthermal varieties because they resist the cold well but not the heat, and the macrothermal (tares and grass) because they love warm climates and lose color at low temperatures.

Among the most suitable botanical varieties, plants that require little light, such as philodendron, ficus, fern, and fatsia, grow on the rocky walls of tropical areas and have therefore demonstrated their specific resistance to extreme situations and conditions.

Building a Vertical Garden: Plant Placement

The positioning of the different species of plants must also consider the micro-climatic conditions, which differ according to the height since. In most cases, the walls rise considerably from the ground.

In fact, temperature and luminosity can be different at the base and the top, providing the growth of one part over the other.

For this reason, plants that require little light and are more resistant to humidity and cold are placed at ground level, where the shade is greater, while sun-loving plants are placed in the brightest and highest part of the wall.

Finally, the chromatic effect is important. The opportunity to combine perennial and seasonal plants allows the already strong impact of the vertical garden to be given new colors and suggestive effects with the passing of the seasons.

Irrigation and Fertilization of a Vertical Garden

They are the fundamental treatments for all the varieties used in vegetable walls. In order to guarantee water and fertilizer, we often should use automatic systems incorporated in the plants via manifolds arranged horizontally at different wall levels.

These collectors are connected to vertical riser pipes that run the length of the infrastructure, providing all the plants with nutrients. If the system uses a closed-cycle irrigation system, the water becomes rainwater stored in collection containers at the base of the wall.

The hydroponic cultivation method was also used, which allows a constant rainwater supply and fertilizers through drip systems put in the upper part of the wall.

Cost of a Vertical Garden

The factors that contribute to the price are many: irrigation system, substrate, materials used for the structure, and essences.

Due to their innumerable benefits, the fabrication of these green walls should be encouraged. Beyond the great works and the wide range of patents available, there still seems to be a lack of a real and widespread design and technical construction capacity.

Despite this, there is great attention towards them: the marketing of prefabricated green panels - already equipped with plants - is becoming a reality.

Benefits of the Vertical Garden

If their aesthetic value is beyond doubt, the plus added to urban spaces by their presence is not only of an ornamental nature.

The city's surface destined for green areas is increasingly reduced, sacrificed by architectural expansion. The green wall is the greenest and most effective response to the problems that afflict modern cities. Its innumerable advantages are that it:

- Offers natural protection from noise pollution, offering a natural barrier to sound.
- Purifies the air by absorbing CO_2 and also cleaning it from smog. And therefore, it contributes to improving air quality by helping to reduce the incidence of respiratory system diseases and saving the health system.
- Insulates buildings, providing excellent insulation that allows energy savings and lowers the energy required to heat and cool them
- offers good fire resistance.
- It gives well-being because the view of a garden, instead of a concrete wall, rests the eye and relaxes the mind
- guarantees a greater balance between concrete and greenery
- increases the value of the property because they make it more beautiful and refined, as well as insulated to respond to the summer heat greenly.

Indoor Vertical Garden

Illustrious examples demonstrate that vertical green is not just something closed and confined.

It undermines the most obvious idea of horizontal growth of greenery and gives life to a myriad of possible solutions, proving to be a winner because it is capable of adapting, in the most creative ways, to the needs dictated by the realities in which it fits.

It can be the decoration of an internal wall of a courtyard, as in the case of the Intercontinental hotel in Paris, or an internal wall of a house, perhaps in the bathroom, to take advantage of the humidity in the environment. Or let's think of a 'green' picture to hang in the living room.

A Vertical Garden on the Balcony

If you have a terrace or a small balcony, it doesn't mean you can't create your vertical garden, perhaps with vegetables to grow even for cooking. Some plants can be grown easily in a small space, which is even more true in the case of a vertical garden.

Again the rule is the same as for large installations: avoid plants that take up too much space or require too much soil depth.

Most aromatic plants are perfect, including lettuce, cherry tomatoes, peppers, onions, radishes, garlic, and strawberries.

Another factor to consider is that it is necessary to water regularly because they are still potted or balcony plants, so the soil dries out quite quickly.

Finally, reserve a sunny position, and you will have more variety of choices.

The simplest solution is to use ladders on which to hang the vases. Better if inclined so as not to shade the plants placed below.

Do-It-Yourself Vertical Garden

There are different types of green walls in mini and do-it-yourself versions for indoors and outdoors. Here are some ideas.

Plant pockets. It can accommodate many plants, both in width and height. These are pockets up to 2 m high that can occupy the entire width of a wall. It is also possible to hang them on a balcony railing, on a solid wire mesh, or a wooden trellis. They can be found on the market in water-repellent and humidity-resistant fabric, sufficiently resistant to the weight of the soil and plants.

Vases. You can keep plants in pots and then hang them from a frame. You can play with the sizes of pots or even use cans with holes in the bottom. Don't hesitate to mix vegetables, aromatic plants, and flowering plants with evergreens. We advise against hanging plastic bottles on threads because a transparent container will cause the roots to dry out quickly.

Pallet. The pallets are used to support, creating spaces in the center or inserting the plants between the slats. Remember to check that the wood contained in the pallet has not been treated with chemicals (especially those intended for storing materials outdoors).

Plant wall. There are felt walls on the market with holes to be fixed to the wall that can accommodate climbing plants in different bands that will fall downwards.

Chapter 3.
BALCONY VEGETABLE GARDENING

B alcony Gardening has been proclaimed trend No. 1 for 2021. A search by Love the Garden, the garden care company Evergreen Garden Care portal, has collected over 100 different hashtags on 'gardening' used by people on Instagram.

Taking precedence over other trends such as Wild Gardens (growing wildflowers in the garden), raised flower beds, or the White Garden (designing one's garden in white hues), this trend has forcefully entered the lives of many of us. What do we mean by Balcony Gardening? Let's go find out.

With Balcony Gardening, we mean the cultivation of plants and vegetables on your balcony or terrace. The pandemic has prompted many people to take advantage of their green thumb directly at home. This is to avoid the worry of going out or the endless lines at the fruit and vegetable shop.

Hence the use of plants, flowers, and vegetable gardens to be planted on the balcony to spend days outdoors in full compliance with the anti-Covid rules, producing tomatoes, courgettes, lettuces, and other products to be used in the kitchen. In this regard, Agricultural associations have highlighted a significant increase in purchases in supermarkets and markets of seedlings, seeds, fertilizers, and gardening tools for home cultivation.

Since there are obviously different balconies, this 2021 trend can be carried forward in other ways through 3 ways of cultivating.

- Vertical garden: if you have unused parts of the wall available and you don't know where to throw your empty plastic bottles, you could use them to grow your seedlings in them. The vertical garden contributes to the recycling of these objects, and developing vertically is the ideal solution for saving space.
- As an alternative to bottles, you can also use small wooden shelves or planters.
- Pots and planters: they are indeed the simplest and most practical solution. Plastic or terracotta pots and the relative saucers are available in several sizes and can be used for any type of seedling.
- Cultivation tables: if you have a lot of space available, choosing a cultivation table will allow you to have a solid support base for the most diverse crops.

What and When To Grow in the Garden

Of the 2021 trends, Balcony Gardening will be one of the most followed. But what should you grow? To cultivate on the balcony, it will first of all be necessary to make targeted choices: it will be required to evaluate the space available and, even more importantly, the exposure of the balcony to the sun's rays.

A north-facing balcony is not the best for growing, while southwest or south-east exposures remain the best condition, provided you avoid the sun during the hottest hours of the day. Finally, it will be necessary to choose the type of soil, which must be rich in nutrients and able to retain water without creating stagnation.

Fortunately, many garden products are perfectly suited to growing in a small space and can therefore be planted in pots. For example, lettuce is one of the most requested plants: it guarantees a harvest after just 40 days, all at a meager price. Another highly appreciated product for ease and timing of harvest is tiny tomato seedlings, although they are a little more expensive than a simple salad.

It will also be necessary to take into account the seasonality of fruit and vegetables:

- winter: oranges, apples, tangerines, lettuce, artichokes, cauliflower, garlic, lemons, chicory, turnips, celery
- spring: kiwis, pears, grapefruit, asparagus, broccoli, carrots, spring onions, radicchio, spinach, turnips
- summer: apricots, cherries, strawberries, raspberries, melons, peaches, figs, plums, cucumbers, green beans, eggplants, peppers, peas, zucchini
- autumn: grapes, persimmons, clementines, raspberries, blueberries, radishes, chard.

Pro tips

To start cultivating your balcony correctly, we provide you with some simple tips below to avoid running into trivial and evaluation errors:

- Using a single large pot, if you have the right space, will allow you to water all your vegetables at once;
- Plants instead of seeds: if your time is precious and you are impatient, the best solution could be to buy the seedlings that have already sprouted and transplant them at home. All this would be best done in the spring;
- Basic soil: starting with the simplest type of soil will be fine to begin with; green light, therefore, to a universal organic ground without peat;
- Mulching: using this technique means covering the surface of the soil with material, such as pieces of bark, gravel, or pebbles, to prevent the growth of weeds, maintain the proper humidity in the soil and protect the soil from erosion.

Thanks to Balcony Gardening, the space on the balcony will be exploited more and more and in an optimal way: the products will be healthier, and your home will be filled with greenery!

Chapter 4.
SHADY VEGETABLE GARDENING

Not all land benefits from the full sun: there are plots facing north and perhaps shaded by plants or buildings. In most gardens, whether in the shade of a tree or near a hedge, there are areas where the sun's rays only arrive at certain times.

These somewhat shady lands can still be cultivated; the crucial thing is to know how to choose the crops suitable for a lower presence of the sun; for this, we will see below which crops can be grown in the shade.

To tell the truth, no vegetables can be kept in complete shade, but we can instead take advantage of the so-called partial shade areas, where the sun's rays arrive only for a few hours a day.

The sun is certainly a fundamental element for plants; just think that chlorophyll photosynthesis takes place thanks to light. For this reason, no plant in the garden can live without it. However, there are crops that are satisfied with less exposure, while others give their best only if they receive many hours of direct sunlight.

What to Grow in Shady Vegetable Garden

If you have a plot facing north or a part of the vegetable garden where the hedge creates shade, do not plant peppers or tomatoes: it is important to choose vegetables that are less demanding in terms of sunlight.

There are salads such as lettuce, chicory, and rocket that can be satisfied in a particularly shady place; even garlic, spinach, ribs, herbs, fennel, carrots, celery, pumpkins, and courgettes do not necessarily require full sun. Among cabbages, kohlrabi is the most suitable for shaded areas.

Some of these horticultural plants that I have listed would be better if they were grown in full sun, but if you are satisfied with a slightly less rich harvest and with slightly longer ripening times, you can still plant them, thus managing to use land that otherwise they would not have been cultivable.

In addition to vegetables, you can choose aromatic plants that can stay in places with little sun: thyme, sage, mint, lemon balm, tarragon, and parsley will not suffer too much. Small fruits can be grown in partial shade, such as gooseberries, currants, blueberries, and strawberries: let's not forget that these plants are born in nature as 'berries' and are therefore used to being in the shade of larger trees.

Pro Tips

- Never in full shade. Plants need light: it must be known that if the ground is completely in the shade, it will not be possible to grow vegetables with appreciable results. We have seen that there are less demanding vegetable plants, but all of them should have a minimum of 4 or 5 hours of sun a day. It is not possible to grow vegetables completely in the shade.

- Transplant rather than sow. In the initial stage of a plant's life, in which the seed germinates and then develops a small seedling, the sun is very important. When it is missing, the young seedlings develop badly: they lose color, produce very small leaves and grow slender in height; it is commonly said that "plants spin." For this reason, it is advisable to have them born in a correctly lit seedbed and then transplant them in the partial shade area 45/60 days after sowing. This does not apply to carrots, a vegetable that suffers a lot if it is transplanted.

- Beware of the cold. The sun brings not only light but also heat; for this reason, land in partial shade is often more subject to frosts, and the temperatures will be lower than in sunny positions. When planning cultivation, it is vital to consider this factor to prevent frost from ruining the vegetables.

- Beware of humidity. The scarcity of the sun leads to less evaporation of water; for this reason, the shaded soil tends to remain more humid. On the one hand, this is positive, irrigation is saved, but it could also be an easy viaticum for fungi, molds, and diseases in general. To avoid this, you need to work the soil well during the planting phase so that it drains well, and weed it often during cultivation, thus oxygenating the earth.

Vegetables that can be grown in a shady garden:

- Zucchini;
- Fennel;
- Lettuce;
- Carrots;
- Celery;
- Swiss chard;
- Soncino;
- Garlic;
- Spinach;
- Rocket salad;
- Radishes;
- Cutting chicory;
- Pumpkins.

Chapter 5.
CONTAINER VEGETABLE GARDENING

Do you live in an apartment or a smaller lot? Think you don't have enough garden space? Well, whatever your situation, I'm here to tell you about one way you could potentially grow your own food.

Are you familiar with the expression «container gardening»? If not, I'll introduce it to you today.

So let's start exploring the concept of container gardening.

What is Container Gardening?

Container gardening is a simple concept, even if it's relatively new to most of us. Essentially, you have several containers and grow individual plants in each one.

You may think you can't grow anything in a container, but that's the case. It is that simple. If you have a few buckets or pots and a sunny spot, you can grow a small garden in individual containers.

I prefer container gardening, in my experience. We have an ample garden space, but I still grow several items in a container each year as I think they are easier to maintain.

For example, I grow my colorful pepper varieties in containers every year. I also grow my carrots in containers.

If you have a fun place for a pot garden, you should give it a try. The upfront cost is minimal, and you might just find your new favorite hobby.

How Can Container Gardening Help Me?

I understand that not everyone can grow a garden, even a potted garden. When I was younger, single, and just getting started, I used to live in a small studio apartment with my cat.

And when I say tiny, it was a tiny little apartment. But it didn't even have a balcony. I probably could have used a side yard near my building, but I wasn't thinking about gardening at the time.

So I understand that a potted garden isn't for everyone, but if you have a small patio or even a balcony, it might be just right for you.

This means that a container garden can be beneficial in one way or another. You may think you can't get a big harvest out of containers, but it really is possible. I grow enough carrots for my family in about five pots.

So you don't need to have a lot of space to get a big harvest. This crop provides fresh, good-for-you food at a fraction of the cost.

Plus, you know what you're eating because you're the one lifting it.

Nor should we forget those who have a more extensive garden but cannot physically get there.

You don't (necessarily) have to give up gardening completely. If you can get out onto your back porch, you may be able to grow things in containers.

Then there are people like me. I'm doing a container garden on top of a large garden because, I have better luck with containerized vegetables. I always have a hard time growing carrots in the garden, but I do very well in a container. I can keep the soil loose enough that they grow easier.

I have also found that repotting can spare your plants some of the disease problems they may encounter if planted in a wider garden. This is usually due to the space between plants, as they do not feed on the same soil.

As you can see, container gardening has many benefits for virtually everyone.

What Can You Grow in a Container Garden?

As stated above, one might think that container gardening doesn't mean much.

Well, I'm here to tell you that if you think so, then you are wrong. We can grow a variety of vegetables in containers. Don't forget that you can buy seeds to put in containers. This might make container gardening a little easier if you're new to it.

So here are some items you can grow in containers:

Corn

I know, the first time I saw corn growing in a container, I had to do a double take. But it can work.

And I was pleased to see how beautiful corn looks when grown in a container. You could easily put it on your porch or balcony for some decoration, as well as for eating.

Tomatoes

Growing tomatoes in a container is a breeze. I find my tomatoes feel a little better in a container because I tend to take better care of them.

For example, we plant large quantities of red tomatoes in our garden every year. However, I like yellow tomatoes, so I usually plant a few in containers to enjoy and save some for canning.

Strawberries

I grow my strawberries in containers every year. My strawberries are planted around an old tree trunk that was once a widowmaker.

So we cut old plastic kegs in half, filled them with soil, and planted strawberries. Every year they get bigger and bigger.

Fruit Trees

That's how I got the courage to have an orchard. I had read and heard all these things about fruit trees, and I knew I loved them, but I was intimidated by them.

So one year we went to Florida and I bought little orange and lemon trees at a gift shop. Then I brought them home and raised them in containers. This is how my orchard was born… in a container.

Green Beans

Green beans can easily be grown in a container. You'll have to use a wild bean for this to work really well (in my experience) because then they'll collapse instead of running around.

However, if you prefer runners to shrubs, I'm sure you could put some trellises in the pot to give them something to run on.

Pumpkin

Pumpkin is another plant that would probably need a small trellis inserted into the container to provide a place to grow.

However, squash is a fairly simple vegetable to grow, with various varieties.

Melons

Melons are another option that may not be immediately considered when considering container gardening.

But they can also grow in a container with a trellis structure.

Carrots

As I said, I prefer container-growing carrots. I think it's easier because it's easy to make sure the soil stays loose.

However, I grow mine in large pots, so they have plenty of room to grow. Remember to thin out the carrots as they begin to sprout, and make sure they grow in a large (and deep enough) container.

Potatoes

Potatoes are another plant that I have found to grow quite easily in a container. We always tend to plant most of our potatoes in the ground to get a bigger crop.

Onions

Onions are another that can be container grown because it's easier to move around as needed.

In fact, I usually have better luck with onions in containers too, because that way, I can put them where I need them to keep my chickens away!

Garlic

Garlic is another commodity that can be grown in containers. Growing them takes time, so planting them in containers can make it easier to find a place to grow them.

I also find it easier to keep my chickens off the garlic using this method as well.

Peppers

I grow a few peppers in containers every year. Our large garden has one row for normal peppers and another row for hot peppers.

But I also like growing a variety of colors in peppers. So I will plant my colorful peppers in containers for them to enjoy and take care of as well.

Pro Tips: How To Start

Starting a container garden does not require large investments. You probably have most items close at hand.

This is what you will need to create your potted garden:

1. <u>Containers</u>

There is no need to invent pots for a potted garden. We grow most of our items in big old pots that I don't use for anything else.

Also, I use a lot of five-gallon buckets. My husband went through this stage of collecting every bucket he could find.

However, it worked out perfectly for me because I poked holes in the bottom of most of them just to allow the water to drain correctly, and then planted them (everyone knows you need to be a patient man to put up with my pranks!)

But if I find myself short (because I went too far in the planting, as usual), I use plastic pots.

2. <u>Good soil</u>

Then they will need good soil for their plants to grow. You can purchase the soil at any local garden center.

Or you can create your grand plan. We have a place on my mother-in-law's property that we dug up. It's a place in the woods, and I don't know why it's so big, but she's always told us to use the land there, and we've been doing it for years.

Finding a great floor is, therefore, not too difficult a task. Even if you have to buy land and can't afford the large variety (because it's expensive), use some tips to improve it.

3. <u>A sunny spot</u>

Once they have their pots and good soil, they will need a sunny spot to plant. It can be a back porch, front porch, side yard, balcony, or even a sunny window. It is possible to grow some herbs in containers on the windowsill.

Once you have a sunny spot in mind, you are almost ready to start your container garden.

4. <u>Seeds to Plant</u>

The last thing you will need to create your pot garden. I will explain later how to find seeds for practically nothing.

So, once you have the strains you want to plant, plant them in good soil in your container in a sunny spot, and away you go.

Chapter 6.
SCALE VEGETABLE GARDENING

At least 800 million people suffer from non-world hunger. For this reason, 'let's wake up before it's too late' is an invitation, but also the title of a United Nations report which indicates one of the keys to reversing this terrible situation: small-scale ecological agriculture.

If this line were to be imposed, which would require a 180-degree turn in industry and international trade policy, we would make enormous progress toward food sovereignty. For this, it would also be necessary to support farmers who encounter enormous difficulties accessing seeds and selling their products.

In this way, we could begin to give a concrete response to the people who suffer from chronic hunger in the world or those who do not reach this extreme but are still malnourished.

What, then, is meant by a small-scale vegetable garden?

We all would like a large vegetable garden full of products that give us sustenance 365 days a year. Well, it is possible to achieve this important result even with a small-scale vegetable garden, or rather a fully functional and self-sufficient vegetable garden capable of exploiting small spaces for maximum yield.

Let's see together how to build a vegetable garden on a small-scale.

Pots, Hanging Baskets, Pergolas, Blooms, Kitchen Window Boxes, Containers... You can choose any of these containers to start building a small-scale vegetable garden.

Vegetables grown in pots, bowls, and crates or small spaces in the garden are a guarantee of flavor and health and can be splendid and generous in every season of the year, concentrating great opportunities for environmental sustainability in just a few square meters. They are also opportunities for socializing, recovering ethical values, and healthy and genuine 'zero km' flavors.

As well as the vegetable garden on the balcony, the small-scale garden, once a classic refuge for the pensioner who often went to use abandoned spaces near the railways and on the edge of the city, today constitutes an important small-scale alternative to large-scale intensive agriculture based on forced cultivation rhythms based on an entrepreneurial logic of maximum yield per hectare in terms of production, goods and therefore profit.

Small-scale and balcony gardens today concentrate in a few square meters of great opportunities for environmental sustainability, occasions for socialization and recovery of values, and express an aesthetic meaning that is articulated throughout the seasons.

What to Grow

Many vegetable plants are also perfectly suited to life in pots, as long as they are large and deep, allowing you to savor home-grown vegetables on a daily or almost daily basis. Of course, you must choose species and varieties that require little land to develop roots. Practically of every type of vegetable, it is possible to find at least one dwarf or space-saving variety; some, such as cabbage, require a certain space, but you can decide to keep even just one or two for the aesthetic aspect and for a small but interesting harvest of crunchy and tasty leaves.

Choosing the Best Containers

To cultivate vegetables such as head lettuce, onions, and turnips, tanks of at least 100 x 50 x 50 cm needed to be kept in full sun, filled with good new and fertile land; today, there are also bags of specific soil for vegetable species.

Choose deep containers and ensure drainage by spreading a layer of clay marbles on the bottom; cover the clay with a piece of the non-woven sheet before spreading the soil to prevent the two materials from mixing and the soil from coming out of the drainage holes, with the risk of clogging them.

Purchasing Seedlings

To leave without difficulty, especially in summer, and at the end of summer to make an autumn vegetable garden, it is advisable to buy ready-made seedlings, which always give good results. The decision to start with the seedlings, available in garden centers, local markets, and supermarkets, allows you to have the potted garden ready immediately, taking advantage of their greater resistance compared to the specimens of seedlings obtained from seed cultivation, and avoiding taking up space with greenhouses or seed trays.

Irrigation

The potted garden requires daily watering. The automatic drip system is useful to keep the substrate constantly moist. The waterings are to be done early in the morning or evening and in quantities proportionate to moistening the soil without excesses.

If you water with a watering can, remove the onion and pour the water only gently near the stem of the plants.

Make sure that there are several hours of sunshine in the location chosen for the potted garden, especially if you also want to cultivate in the winter months.

Fertilization

In pots, it is necessary to fertilize abundantly with products suitable for vegetable plants. A useful choice: Gesal BIO universal organic fertilizer, easy to distribute, nourishes for up to 5 months. It has an immediate fertilizing effect and a long-lasting nourishing effect, up to 5 months; it retains water and helps plants better cope with dry periods.

Distribute the fertilizer evenly over the soil, which must already be a little damp, not dry; Incorporate the granules into the soil by raking gently and watering the plants. Dose: 30-50 g of fertilizer every 30 cm of the length of the planters; for other needs, see the instructions on the package.

The Topping of Vegetables

Both to favor production and because on the terrace, the aesthetic side has its importance, check the plants often to trim tomatoes and peppers (i.e., remove the apical shoot to favor flowering), tie the shoots to the wooden or bamboo stakes, check that the lettuce does not go into flower (the production of tender leaves would end), and to make sure that there are no parasites. Every day, check which vegetables are ready for harvesting: in the height of summer, production is daily.

Pest Control

Monitor the health of the foliage and fruits and, where necessary, intervene exclusively with products allowed in organic farming: you will bring the vegetables to the table. Therefore it is better to move towards products of natural origin to be used by carefully following the instructions on the label.

9 Tips for Having Vegetables All Year Round

Sow in a protected environment (seed tray, greenhouse) as early as autumn or January.

Sowing and transplanting must be staggered throughout the season to prolong the productivity of each group of vegetables as much as possible.

If there is little space, it is better to plant only 3-5 specimens of each variety, choosing different varieties both to have different flavors and according to harvest times. This is especially true for lettuces, radicchio, and summer vegetables such as tomatoes and aubergines.

Get yourself a small greenhouse or tunnel kit for winter and spring; without this precaution, the vegetable garden remains devoid of vegetables from January to March and from November onwards.

Some autumn-harvested vegetables, such as cabbage and savoy cabbage, are sown or bought in sprouts in the summer for a transplant that must not take place after August; if it is very hot, a shade cloth is needed over the seedlings.

Leafy vegetables are available in virtually any season; for the winter, think of chard, rocket, endive, radicchio, and valerian.

Some vegetables, such as Brussels sprouts and turnips, are also harvested under the snow.

Summers are now very hot and dry; to protect the crop, in addition to the shading nets, provide a small drip system, which saves water and keeps the soil well moist but not soaked.

Expect something special for every season: wild strawberries in spring, peanuts in summer, alchechengi in autumn, beetroot in winter…

5 Tips for Potted Herbs

Don't forget the aromatic herbs: many species offer leaves to be harvested all year round and are indispensable for flavoring dishes and preparing herbal teas; moreover, they help to keep insects and mosquitoes away thanks to their aroma.

Aromatic herbs grow well in pots and boxes if the containers are deep and well drained: stagnant water in the saucer causes root rot for a long time.

Almost all aromatics require at least 4-6 hours of sun. Basil, lemon balm, and mint are satisfied with very airy and bright positions with little sun.

Gesal is used to fertilize aromatic herbs. BIO Aromatics & Chillies Liquid Fertilizer: perfect product for the care of aromatic plants and chilies; it guarantees tastier leaves and fruits with nourishment allowed in organic farming; contains nutrients of natural origin. Gives adequate crunchiness to the leaves and increases the flavor and color of the fruit. Easy dosing without waste: graduated cap with drip catcher

If you want to compose large vases or mixed bowls with different aromatics, avoid putting sage and rosemary in the same container; good, however, a composition with sage, thyme, oregano or rosemary, marjoram, and fennel.

Chapter 7.
RAISED BED VEGETABLE GARDENING

A raised garden bed is a garden covering that, as the name suggests, is raised off the ground. Many gardeners praise their useful traits! A raised bed makes checking the health of the soil much easier as it allows you to create a more controllable environment. Another reason gardeners love raised beds is the height of the flowers. They are much taller than they would if they grew out of the ground, allowing viewers to see them better.

This also makes it easier for you to work on those plants! Not only do you have less work because the terrain is more accessible, but you don't even have to keep bending over! Working the land is much cheaper.

Some experts suggest that raising plants off the ground will solve problems with problematic soil, such as clay or sand. There are also far fewer surface issues you should worry about.

Finally, we have to mention parasites. There are many animals that can only eat your plants if they are at ground level. If you use a raised bed, this is not a problem.

How to Start

Fall or early spring are the best seasons to set up a raised bed. First, set the base area. So that you can garden comfortably, the bed should be 80-120cm high and no wider than 130cm. The length depends on personal preferences but also on the stability of the building material used. A minimum length of 200 to 250 centimeters is recommended so that you can enter the earth exchange and the Kompode soil can easily shovel out from the inside. Note, however, that longer sidewalls bend more easily and may need to be reinforced with stakes. Spread the flooring over the entire bed area about 10 inches deep, then poke or hollow out four wooden posts at the corner points.

Building Material

Wood is the most common building material for raised beds.

For high walls, various building materials come into question. Mostly strong wooden boards are used, which are fastened with wood screws on the outside of the corner posts. If you are using thinner wooden planks, you must stabilize the side walls outside with more wooden posts rammed vertically into the ground. Use wood that is as weather and rot-resistant as possible. Suitable are oak, larch, and douglas, as well as various tropical woods, which should, however, come from certified forests. Fir or spruce wood is only suitable if pressure impregnated.

Stone For a Permanent Building

Stone is also an excellent building material for raised beds. It is completely weatherproof, mildew resistant, and has relatively heat-insulating properties. Important is a concrete foundation that goes up to 80 centimeters. Anyone who has never even masonry should avoid taking big hole clinker or lime sandstone - so they go the quickest and easiest.

Raised beds are very present in the garden depending on their size and should therefore be adapted to the rest of the garden design. Furthermore, they can serve as a demarcation or room divider.

A Metal Raised Bed

Metal is also used as a building material for raised beds. Suitable, for example, galvanized corrugated sheets are screwed to four wooden corner posts. The corrugated profile ensures good stiffening so that the plates do not bend even under high pressure on the ground. Small drawback: the metal conducts heat and cold very well, so in the colder months, the decomposition process can be delayed.

Installation Advice

There are two important details to consider when building a raised bed. On the one hand, you should coat the interior walls with tin lining, so they do not touch the decaying material.

This is especially true for raised beds in timber construction, but also on stone walls, it is an important cladding. It prevents moisture from seeping through the stone, making it unsightly. The second important measure is a tight wire mesh, which is spread over the entire surface before the walls are installed: it prevents the entry of vole mice.

The right soil layers in the raised bed

The high yield of raised beds is mainly due to the lower soil layers, which consist of garden waste such as branches and foliage. Decomposition processes in the newly filled raised bed to generate heat and raise the soil temperature by up to 5-8 degrees Celsius. Plants grow faster, and the growing season takes longer. On the other hand, many nutrients are released during decomposition, so we can usually dispense with the additional fertilizer. An additional supply of nutrients comes from the carbon dioxide gas released on the rump, which slowly rises through the loose soil and, like the other nutrients, is important for plant growth.

Layer by Layer

Fill the finished bed in layers: each layer should be 25 to 30 centimeters thick. The material is getting finer from the bottom up. The base is made up of rough branches and branches. They ensure that the green waste is well-ventilated from below and can decompose evenly. So that the material stacked on top does not pass through, it is better to cover the shrub cut with a sod of inverted grass. The next layer consists of semi-decomposed and finer plant remains, such as shredded shrubs, autumn leaves, and shrubs. Finally, apply a layer of mature compost or humus and fill it to the brim.

Choosing The Plants

Most vegetables thrive well in the raised bed; only large species such as squash, rhubarb, or zucchini you should do better. Rich crops produce mixed crops, such as cucumbers with dill, carrots with onions, or beans with savory. The nasturtium brings colorful splashes of color to the game and lets its decorative tendrils hang on the walls.

If the berry bushes are planted higher up, the harvest will be easier, and the berries will not lie on the ground, where they will easily become soggy and rotten.

In the first year, the nutrient supply of the plants is so good that only vegetables that do not consume much and do not accumulate nitrates in the leaves and fruits should be grown. Leeks, aubergines, tomatoes, cucumbers, or cabbage are very suitable. From the third year, you can also plant low-energy herbs and lettuce.

Plant Care

The soil sinks if the plant remains in the raised bed and slowly rots. Therefore, it is necessary to refill compost before each new sowing if necessary. After five or six years, it is necessary to completely replace the bedding. The existing organic material has completely decomposed until then and has released almost all the nutrients to the crops. The old soil gives good humus and can be used for soil improvement in the vegetable garden or perennial flower bed.

Effortless Gardening

In summer, water the bed abundantly and regularly. The loose structure dries the soil faster than the normal vegetable garden. Tip: The bed should be within range of the garden hose. So watering is easy, and you don't need to carry watering cans. Even against slugs, raised beds have been proven. You can simply mount it on the top edge or in the middle of a circumferential, angled steel plate edge so your young greens are safe from voracious reptiles.

Ornamental Gardens

Raised beds are not only suitable for extending the season in the vegetable garden. They are also increasingly used in garden design, for example, to divide the plot, surround a seat, or bridge height differences in the garden. So that these ornamental beds also meet the optical requirements, using them for the side walls, for example, natural stones, clinker, or decorative wooden boards, is recommended. You don't need special layering like in vegetable gardening; just fill the raised beds with humus-rich garden soil for planting small woody plants such as fan maple, azalea, or bellflower and almost all perennials.

Chapter 8.
VEGGIE VEGETABLE GARDENING

The veggie garden pays particular attention to vegetables; courgettes, kale, and tomatoes are just some of the delicacies that this garden can give us. One of the solutions to better appreciate this type of cultivation could be represented by the home garden, that precious piece of land of which our grandparents were so proud and which today could become a valid compromise in favor of our health and that of the whole planet. Let's see together how to build it!

When and Where to Start

The first symptoms of spring are the ideal time to start this new experience.

The most suitable place would obviously be a small garden, the classic terrace could also be fine: even if in this case the spaces will be greatly reduced (as we have seen for the small-scale vegetable garden).

A solution to this last problem is that of sharing with a relative or friend; alternatively, social or urban gardens are also good, as they are already operational in many countries. The dimensions are certainly important, but even a small space is enough to get started to practice.

Composting

Once the space has been identified, it will be necessary to plan the organization of composting, which can be obtained from the same waste deriving from lunch and dinner (also strictly vegetable) and contained in a normal wooden box.

After all, 'home composting' is a fairly well-known practice: to start, just get a bin with a lid, some soil, two nets, and some expanded clay that will be placed on the bottom.

Now arrange the nets on the bottom and inside sides of the bin, then drill holes and secure them to the structure using wire.

A Help from the Worms

The veggie diet is very rich in vegetables and fruit: the composting, therefore, will take place in a completely natural way thanks to the earthworms that will feed on the peels and waste leaves. The more the production of our veggie garden goes on, the more the composting will be enriched by waste; in this way, the contents of the bin will be diversified.

Using Hops

Other alternatives to produce compost independently can be to use a particular fertilizer obtained from hops or total vegetables or to exploit the properties of lithothamnium, a product obtained from red algae particularly rich in magnesium and calcium; green manures could also be used.

Seeds

Now there remains the question of seeds. For example, seeds that come from organic crops can be used; barters can be made with other do-it-yourself growers, taking advantage of the seed savers network. Or, much more simply, start conserving the seeds of the products that are consumed and learn how to grow and save them. We will discuss it in detail in Book 6.

Transplanting and Seeding

Transplanting and sowing will be carried out in compliance with natural cycles, very early in the morning or during the evening; alternatively, it could be easier to use seedlings and then transfer the seedlings to the garden.

Irrigation

By adhering to the veggie philosophy, we will try to avoid wasting water, perhaps preferring a 'drop by drop' type of irrigation that we can easily make by making holes along the entire length of the tube.

Fighting against Parasites

Also beware of the sworn enemies of the garden, such as weeds. The use of herbicides is prohibited, and the mulching method is much more appropriate. This method involves the use of inert material to cover the soil, keeping it moist and away from weeds and weeds; mulching will reduce the penetration of winter frost by protecting the roots and allowing us to water less frequently.

Another enemy that should not be underestimated is represented by parasites. Also, in this case, we will avoid the use of pesticides, preferring remedies that may appear somewhat strange but which certainly work, as well as being completely natural.

The first trick will be to scatter heads of garlic in the garden, which is excellent protection against insects; alternatively, we can prepare a type of natural pesticide at home by chopping four cloves of garlic and adding two teaspoons of mineral oil after letting everything rest for a whole night we will remove the garlic, add a glass of water and a teaspoon of organic soap. Other solutions could be represented by a paper or baking soda to combat mold.

The Harvest

We have thus arrived at the most awaited and rewarding moment: the harvest.

During the harvest, avoid tearing the fruits or plants with your hands, this is because some of them have the characteristic of regenerating themselves (salads for example), which cannot happen if they are brutally uprooted.

Chapter 9.
NO-DIG HYDROPONIC VEGETABLE GARDENING

No-dig is a 'no-cultivation' method widely used in small-scale horticulture. In this system, the soil is never worked, there is no hoeing, no milling, and, above all, the soil layers are not reversed with plowing.

The origins of this method are unclear, but among the first pioneers, we can name Masanobu Fukuoka, Ruth Stout, and A. Guest, who, in 1948, wrote the book 'Gardening without digging.'

There are various ways to get to have cultivation soil soft enough to allow sowing or transplants without previous tillage; some include compost, hay, straw, wood chips, cover sheets, and green manure.

Let's see together how to implement this system for your vegetable garden.

Historically tillage has been used to remove weeds and create a portion of soil soft enough to accommodate a seed or plant; furthermore, by working, the soil is aerated, and it is possible to incorporate fertilizers or crop residues.

However, when we look at the soil from the point of view of microbiology, this appears to us as a dense network of connections between various microorganisms whose role is to recycle nutrients, prevent diseases, solubilize minerals, and form aggregates.

When we go to work on the land, many of these connections are broken, and the general microbial activity is reduced.

Furthermore, the oxygen incorporated in the soil triggers oxidative processes, which lead to the release into the atmosphere of a part of the organic substance in the form of carbon (CO_2).

Another non-negligible factor, which occurs after the plowing of agricultural land, is the erosion of the soil caused by atmospheric agents, mainly the rains which, falling abundantly on the freshly plowed fields, therefore devoid of roots, wash away these lands, effectively reducing the number of nutrients present in the soil.

Regenerative agriculture seeks to look at our agricultural systems differently and to mimic what happens in natural ecosystems.

The no-dig method responds very well to the fundamental principles of regenerative agriculture: to disturb the soil as little as possible, always keep the soil covered and always leave the roots in the ground.

We must immediately specify that 'disturbing the soil as little as possible,' even with a no-dig approach, does not mean not disturbing it at all.

Soil, being a living organism, is in constant motion, always in a dynamic flux of disturbance and response. Among the causes of disruption, there is the movement of the macrofauna, atmospheric events, the harvest of plants, or, for example, even pulling up a weed.

The no-dig method minimizes the amount of disturbance and is the result of careful observation of natural dynamics.

Ecological Successions

In nature, what looks most like one of our freshly milled fields could be a landslide.

What happens when you create a significant disturbance is that you go back to the early stages of ecological succession, from bare ground to a stable ecosystem.

Many seeds receive the signal to germinate, and herbaceous pioneer plants begin to colonize the soil, die, and decompose, creating the ideal conditions for other types of plants to find fertile ground and so on, through herbaceous perennials, shrubs, trees, up to a stable ecosystem such as an oak forest could be.

Our cultivated horticultural crops, although they are to all intents and purposes 'selected weeds', do not belong to that phase of succession in which weeds dominate but rather to an intermediate stage in which pioneer weeds have already fulfilled their task, increasing the level of organic matter and balancing the populations of fungi and bacteria.

In this ecosystem, the soil is disturbed little or not at all. Taking inspiration from these dynamics, we can create an agricultural system that best suits our vegetables and also simplifies our work.

Various Approaches

If you have already heard of no-dig, you certainly associate it with the huge use of compost; horticulturists such as Charles Dowding and Richard Perkins have, in fact, made famous this way of gardening, which involves the use of a layer of at least 10 cm of compost.

What you do with this method is very simple: you cut all the spontaneous vegetation, you put a layer of cardboard sheets (optional), you proceed with 10/15 cm of compost, and you transplant or sow directly into the compost.

This jumps the ground into a more advanced stage of ecological succession, where organic matter is abundant, and the ratio of bacteria to fungi is more balanced. In this way, weed growth is minimal due to the darkening offered by the compost layer and because the weeds thrive in a predominantly bacterial environment.

The system just described offers some advantages, but the sustainability of such massive use of compost is questioned; moreover, not all areas allow it to be found, or it is found but of inferior quality.

Even the self-production of massive quantities of compost is not feasible on a small scale, i.e., within one's own company.

Undoubtedly having a weed-free vegetable garden and an easy-to-work substrate, as far as sowing is concerned, is a plus for any horticulturist. Still, the critical issues have prompted some growers to look for alternative systems that do not involve the use of compost.

Creative Solutions

The goal is to have soil soft enough to be able to transplant our plants without resorting to tillage.

Let me give you an example that happened to me personally.

After carrying out soil analyzes and having ascertained that the ratio between magnesium and calcium was slightly unbalanced, even though the native soil tends to be sandy-loamy, and taking into consideration the materials we had locally available, we acted as follows: at the end of autumn, we spread gypsum (calcium sulfate) on the ground, to rebalance the calcium-magnesium ratio, rock dust, wood chips produced on the farm and manure in such proportions as to have a carbon-nitrogen ratio of 30:1.

Following heavy rain, we covered all the ground with tarps and let the microbiology do its work.

About four months later, we removed the sheets and found such soft ground that we could walk on it with our arm, almost up to the elbow, without any effort.

At this point, we slightly disturbed the soil with the grelinette to aerate deeply, carried out our transplants, covered it with hay, and subsequently, the soil was never touched again.

In our case, this system worked very well, but this does not mean that it can be transported to any other context. There are no copy-and-paste solutions, and every decision must be taken after careful observation.

The Issue of Blackout Cloths

Concealment cloths are certainly a great resource when you want to approach no-dig because they allow you to clean up weeds from the land without mechanical work.

On the other hand, however, the negative side is that they are still made of plastic (average life of about ten years). When we spread large portions of them on the ground, we somehow prevent the natural breathing of the soil. The microbial community is modified in favor of anaerobic and facultative microorganisms.

From the point of view of microbiology, they are not harmful; on the contrary, we should note that in the surface layer, the microbial and macrofauna activity increases; however, the problem of sustainability regarding the use of plastic materials remains.

Sustainability

These last considerations lead us to approach the no-dig technique with a more sustainable method, perhaps even more regenerative, which consists in sowing green manure and, at the time of flowering, enticing it by creating a natural mulch.

This system, in addition to working very well, offers several advantages, including reduced use of plastic materials, live cover that actively feeds microorganisms during the winter, and no need to add other material to mulch.

However, it is not a method that we can always use; for example, in spring, it is not possible to have green manure developed enough to be able to entice it, and since it has not yet gone into flowering, even if it is tempted early it would still have enough energy to get up again.

In Summary

As mentioned earlier, the no-dig method should not be taken as a dogma. Our role within ecosystems is that of disturbers, but we just have to learn to disturb strategically.

It is very common for those who practice no-dig to carry out the first tillage of the soil with the tiller and then stop working it again.

In summary, there are different methods of doing no-dig agriculture, and many companies that espouse this philosophy usually apply a mix of approaches.

For crops such as carrots, a generous layer of compost allows the passage of the seeders and greatly delays the growth of weeds, giving a great advantage to the cultivation. Furthermore, in spring, it offers more incredible warmth due to the black color of the compost, which captures the sun's rays; during the summer, mulching with hay or straw instead refreshes the soil and stops evapotranspiration.

Working with green manure, we satisfy both the need to actively feed the microorganisms and enrich the soil and the need to cover for our transplants.

Finally, as far as soil health is concerned, the no-dig method is undoubtedly the most suitable, and in disadvantaged areas, it dramatically reduces the effort and cost of having to constantly move heavy vehicles.

Tillage is the leading cause of the erosion of our soils: it releases CO_2 into the atmosphere and destroys the soil structure and microbial communities. The only reason why they are still primarily carried out is that, currently, by some farmers, there is too little attention given to regenerative approaches to agriculture.

This does not mean that in some cases, tillage of the soil is not beneficial, perhaps only of the first 5 cm and with suitable tools, but for all the reasons listed above, many farmers are switching to this method, and others are trying to work with 'minimum processing.'

Very often, however, what prevents us from changing our impact on the ecosystem is not the impossibility of switching to alternative methods but the difficulty we find in changing our mental approach; phrases like 'it's always been done like this, 'this thing doesn't work in my field,' 'this is not possible, reflect an attitude of closure and hinder growth.

When we change our mindsets, we see problems, including failures, as opportunities to improve, learn new things, and maybe even become better farmers.

The Hydroponic Way

What is Hydroponic Farming? It is the cultivation of plants without soil, i.e., without soil and thanks to water, in which nutrients suitable for making plants proliferate and healthy are dissolved. In short, it is growing plants in water and identifies using water for cultivating decorative plants and fruit and vegetable. Being a method that doesn't use soil, it's naturally a no-dig.

Let's see now how exactly hydroponic agriculture crops are structured and implemented.

When we talk about Hydroponics, it must be specified that for this type of cultivation, there are techniques that differ significantly from traditional agriculture since the soil is not used.

We can divide this large group of agriculture into two subsets:

- Hydroponic Agriculture with Substrate;
- Hydroponic Agriculture without Substrate.

Hydroponic Agriculture with Substrate

By Hydroponic Agriculture with Substrate, we mean the type of agriculture that uses a substrate to absorb the water and all the nutrients it contains.

This substrate can be made up of mixtures such as expanded clay, perlite, vermiculite, coconut fiber, rock wool, zeolite, and many others.

The substrate, as previously mentioned, will take care of absorbing all the (primarily inorganic) substances that the plant needs to grow strong and luxuriant.

Hydroponic Agriculture without Substrate

Hydroponic Agriculture without Substrate means that type of cultivation is carried out only with water.

The roots of the plants will be completely immersed in the water, and it will be the latter, without the aid of any substrate, that will pass all the nutritional elements needed by the plant.

Very often, certain types of plants, such as rice or carnivorous plants, adapt very well to this hydroponic agriculture without substrate. Others, however, which are the majority, need much more oxygen to grow without problems.

If the plant does not receive the right amount of oxygen in the roots, it risks withering or even dying from asphyxiation. A good rule is to manage the amount of oxygen that is supplied to the plant so as to guarantee its longevity.

The Advantages of Hydroponic Agriculture

This technique manages to stimulate, and therefore speed up, the growth of plants; therefore, it is good practice for the farmer to take care of perfectly controlling the quantity and dosage of air, water, and mineral salts supplied to the plant.

Are we sure the plant will grow fast? Without a doubt, we will dose the number of nutrients for the plant. The latter will absorb them quickly, thanks to the continuous movement that the roots make in the water.

Another great advantage, perhaps the best, is the possibility of genuinely cultivating anywhere and at any time of the year since we will be the ones to recreate the right climate for the growth of a specific type of plant.

Furthermore, hydroponic cultivation saves a lot on the water used to irrigate the plants since there is a continuous recirculation of the same, and it is always dosed plant by plant. We will manage every single drop of water in the best possible way.

The plants will also benefit, as we will provide the nutrients that the plant requires, no more and no less.

No more chemicals will be used to ward off dangerous animals or to keep weeds from growing in our crops. The cultivations can be done indoors, therefore inside a greenhouse or, if seen in small size, inside one's own home or even room.

Even the environment thanks those who use this type of cultivation since a lot of water is saved, more nutrients than necessary are not used, and the use of herbicides or other types of chemical substances is reduced.

To start this type of agriculture on a large scale, it is necessary to have: structures, looms, electricity, and adequate instruments for the correct growth of the plants.

Furthermore, it will be possible to start this type of agriculture even inside one's own home, perhaps to cultivate herbs (basil or rosemary) or spices.

Chapter 10.
HIGH YIELDING WALL

Very widespread in recent times, especially in the most avant-garde countries, and particularly attentive to the environment, the High Yielding Wall is an installation that hosts compositions of different plants inserted in unique pots and anchored on special panels or hooked directly to the internal or external wall of a building. In fact, vertical gardens adapt to any type of environment: indoors and outdoors, such as private premises, rooms in homes and residences, offices, open spaces, and all other types of public places.

Among the most widespread examples of external vertical gardens, however, we find those created to embellish and decorate entire facades of buildings, dividing and retaining fences, self-supporting walls, or separating panels of any kind and on any type of structure.

Growing in Vertical

The cultivation method adopted for a High Yielding vertical wall is the classic one - with a base of soil rinsed with water by means of a simple sprayer - or the hydroponic drop method, installed in the upper part of the wall, where – instead of universal soil – an inert substrate is used (composed for example of perlite, coconut fiber, expanded clay, etc.). The irrigation water is enriched with nutrients and fertilizers capable of feeding the plants.

There are also other solutions – always based on hydroponic systems – which allow you to adapt to the various surfaces and different types of supports. It is possible to choose between various types of hydroponic gardens – also known as green walls or vertical greenery – which can be adapted according to the various needs.

All the Benefits

What are the benefits and advantages of a high-yielding vertical garden? In addition to embellishing the environment with natural and relaxing colors and making the spaces more welcoming and aesthetically attractive, setting up a vertical green space of this type also allows you to purify the air, lowering the levels of pollution and making it purer. Plants absorb carbon dioxide, the CO_2 present in the air, and generate cleaner air, also guaranteeing thermoregulation.

If the vertical garden is placed outside, moreover, the plants are also able to absorb UV rays and clean the air of the smog generated by cars and polluting nearby buildings.

Furthermore, vertical gardens can offer great acoustic and thermal insulation, generating a natural protective barrier capable of improving the lives of those who live in that space.

Furthermore, thanks to this action of insulation and insulation, also of a thermal type, the vertical green wall manages to lower the need and consumption of energy, both for heating and cooling, and - consequently - also allows for economic savings. Moreover, a green panel offers relaxation, because - thanks to the colors and scents of nature - it helps to rest the eye and relax the body and mind.

Choosing the Plants

The selection naturally varies according to the environmental and climatic characteristics of the area in which it is installed (such as exposure to the house, ventilation, etc.) and by personal preferences and individual needs.

For example - depending on your preferences - you can choose cascading plants, which grow downwards, or climbing plants, which will naturally grow taller; alternatively, you can opt for small evergreen plants, or those with limited growth, to engage a decreased commitment and a low level of maintenance.

For the kitchen or the more recreational rooms of the house, it is also possible to create a space to be dedicated to a vertical garden populated by aromatic herbs, such as rosemary, lavender, sage, and lemon verbena, which - in addition to guaranteeing the presence of a pleasant green composition to the eye – they also spread relaxing and beneficial scents and aromas for a unique experience, capable of dramatically improving the quality of life.

In general, the plants most used for creating vertical gardens are ferns, philodendrons, ficuses, and fatsias, because they are resistant and can live even in difficult conditions.

DIY High Yielding Vertical Wall

If you want to create a vertical garden, it is possible to consult specialized companies, especially if the green wall is to be installed on the facades of buildings or large walls. In addition, if you want to create an internal vertical garden in a room of the house or your office, or an external space in the courtyard or garden, it is possible to use do-it-yourself methods: practical, quick, and cheap.

One of the most practical and recommendable systems for creating a domestic vertical garden is the simplest one, characterized by plant pockets. These are felt panels structured with pockets and created specifically to house various types of vegetables. They are available in various sizes and formats and in variable numbers depending on the available space.

The pockets - made of water and humidity-resistant fabric - can also be hung on other surfaces, such as wooden walls, nets, and balcony railings.

Alternatively - again to create your own DIY vertical garden simply and conveniently - you can use specific pots, designed specifically to be hung vertically. In this case, you can insert a substrate inside these pots; the plants are arranged inside the containers and then hung on the wall with dedicated hooks. Using normal garden pots or transparent plastic bottles is not recommended, as the roots tend to dry out too much.

In some cases - especially if you want to set up vertical green space on the balcony or in the courtyard of the house - it is possible to use pallets, which will act as a support for the plant pots that will be set between one slat and another. For this kind of green wall, it is advisable to pick plants adaptable to the characteristics of wooden benches and capable of bearing fruit useful in the kitchen, such as cherry tomatoes, strawberries, onions, salad, or aromatic herbs.

Chapter 11.
WIDE ROWS VEGETABLE GARDENING

The organization, even in the garden with wide rows, is very important; therefore, it is necessary to prepare the land in the most comfortable way to facilitate the work in the following phases. After all, when a vegetable garden is set up, an operation that should not be underestimated is precisely that of preparing the rows.

Depending on the varieties of vegetables and greens, we will have to make excavations that are suitable for that particular type of seed used since there are some earth products that need to be grouped and buried together, while others require rows for each individual seed.

Let's see how you can make the furrows for the garden in the best possible way and the various types of rows. The materials needed are:

- some sticks;
- the twine;
- the rake;
- the hoe;
- a tube.

Excavation for the Rows

Once the soil has been adequately prepared, the rows are made where the seedlings will be placed. The row can be made with a hoe.

Wide rows parallel to each other must have a distance of about 70 cm.

Once the portion of land in which to make the row has been identified, it is necessary to place two poles, respectively, at the beginning and at the end of the excavation area, to which a cord must be tied. This expedient will allow you to have a guideline while tracing the rows. In the case of superficial crops, a rake with the typical four-pointed shape will suffice, which allows the so-called rain sowing.

If we have to enrich the soil with manure mixed with peat to plant vegetables and greens that require adequate fertilization and good drainage, we must instead make wide and deep rows. For this type of row, a shovel should be used to remove the soil and a large plow.

During excavation operations, attention must be paid to the slope, the row should be traced flat, but if the ground is sloping, then it will have to be made perpendicular to avoid the slope.

To plant tubers, the rows should be made square, while for plants that grow at three hundred and sixty degrees, it is preferable to make a circular shape.

Arranging the Rows

Once the first row has been made, the subsequent ones cannot be traced at random but must be made following logic.

The first factor in evaluating is the size of the plant once it has grown: rows that are too close could create space problems, affecting the prosperity of the plant, or, even worse, it could cause two different plants to come into contact, creating complications, such as example, the intertwining of leaves.

Furthermore, you must never forget to leave a space that facilitates your passage between different rows when your presence is needed to sow, water, and harvest the fruits of your garden.

In the event that the dimensions of your land are limited, it is better to reduce the number of rows to prevent your work from being lost in the long run due to excessive proximity.

A useful expedient to recover a few centimeters is to arrange the plants in a checkerboard pattern in the individual row, thus creating free lateral spaces.

When the row has been drawn, one of the sticks used to draw the straight line can be left in the ground to attach a label indicating the type of plant grown.

The usefulness and functionality of the row are to retain water allowing you to wet the plants effortlessly. If made with care, just place the watering hose at the beginning of the row, fill it with 3/4 cm of water along its entire length and proceed with the next row.

You have to make sure that the banks of the row are not damaged, in case you add more earth on the edges, so you will avoid wasting water.

To make watering even easier, the rows can be linked to each other at the beginning or end so as to create a circuit in which the water can move freely when the hose is placed on it.

The distance between the various rows is essential because if they are too close, the growing plants will suffer from the lack of space, and the product will not develop completely. You have to consider how big the plant should get and thus space out the rows. For the same reason, don't place plants too close together in the same row.

If you have limited space available to optimize it, you can put the various plants in rows offset from each other so as to recover centimeters of the earth.

Do not make the rows too deep; if, for example, the row is used for salads, remember that the leaf part of the plant will grow larger over time, so if you have made the row too deep and narrow, the plant will not be able to develop as wide as it would like.

We must remember to leave the various passages that are needed to pass between the seedlings, water, remove the weeds and collect the products.

The Right Slope

To evenly wet all the seedlings, the bottom of the row must be level. If you have sloping ground, the rows must be perpendicular to the slope.

Making the Rows

You can plant two sticks at the beginning and at the end of the space where you want to make the row and join them with a string so as to have a straight line to follow with the hoe when digging the row.

After you have finished digging and the row is ready, you have to remove one of the two sticks, and on the one that remains, you can stick the envelope of the seed you used or simply a plate with the name of the planted product.

For those plants that grow a lot in all directions (for example, courgette plants), we can also make the rows with a circular shape, so we just need to insert the tube under the vegetation of the plant and fill the basin with water without the least effort.

Watering

The functionality of a row can be deduced from the ability to retain water, ensuring the right hydration of the soil without waste. Therefore, before proceeding with watering, check the banks, which are a fundamental element, because it is up to them to keep the water in the row. If they are ruined, you will have to proceed to reinforce them with more soil.

If the row is well dug and the slope is right, a limited amount of water poured from one side of the row will suffice to ensure uniform watering in the soil.

In cases of excessive slopes or rows that are too long, you can insert a pipe inside the track in the ground, on which to make holes evenly along the entire length, to be fixed with clamps to the ground.

To save water when hydrating the garden further, a path can be created between the rows, creating a connection between them. This continuity will allow the water to pass from one row to another, avoiding the creation of stagnation areas in the event of an overabundance of water.

Chapter 12.
DEEP SOIL VEGETABLE GARDENING

Autumn is an important period for the construction of the deep soil: it is the most suitable period to proceed with the so-called autumnal organic fertilization of the orchard, woody plants, and shrubby plants.

Basic fertilization aims to replenish the resources consumed during the growing season by plants to produce leaves, fruits, and new vegetation. In fact, in autumn, the plants face the final phase of the vegetative cycle, and the last activity they carry out, before dormancy, is to prepare the buds for the next spring season.

These buds must be fed: also because plants have the ability to sense the number of nutrients present in the soil and consequently prepare a greater or smaller number of buds, depending on the level of fertility they find in the soil. Basic fertilization is therefore important so that the plants can plan abundant vegetation for next year and, therefore, an adequate number of buds.

How to Do It

Once the harvest is over, it is important to clean the soil at the base of the plants since dry leaves, rotten fruits, and even weeds can host spores of fungal diseases and parasite eggs. Once

STEVEN DOWDING | THE YEAR-ROUND VEGETABLE GARDENER'S BIBLE [7 BOOKS IN 1]

the soil has been cleared, it is possible to apply basic fertilization.

Products to Use

Normally organic-based fertilizers are used, such as manure. Still, organic-mineral fertilizers can also be used: organic-based products integrated with some mineral elements that organic-based fertilizers do not normally contain. For example, elements such as Potassium, Boron, or Zinc should be accumulated by the plant in advance of the growing season.

Even Iron, which is typically applied when the plant does not turn green, should instead be distributed with a preventive rather than a curative logic. And the best time to apply Iron is precisely autumn: we can proceed before the leaves fall with a good foliar fertilization based on Iron, or we can apply it through a basic fertilization that also contains this element.

We can therefore use pelleted manure or a soil conditioner for basic fertilization for vegetable gardens and orchards.

Pro Tips

The basic fertilization is carried out for the orchard, the hedges, and for the shrubby plants. As far as the garden is concerned, we have to make some distinctions.

The basic fertilization of the garden, in fact, follows the crop cycle and must be carried out 30-45 days before planting the plants.

To improve the performance of the garden, corrective measures or amendments can be made in autumn, but only if necessary.

Suppose the soil is excessively calcareous or sandy or has structural defects. In that case, autumn is the ideal period to introduce those elements which tend to correct the soil structure and are, therefore, preparatory for good cultivation.

Chapter 13.
COMPANION PLANTING

We tend to combine plants based on the blooms' colors without considering their cultural needs. But it is an impulsive choice that generates ephemeral satisfaction, the moment of a poppy that fades and causes prolonged problems of coexistence. For example, a hellebore and a verbena will hardly get along: the first love cool and shady areas, and the second thrives in sunny and very well-drained soils.

On the contrary, the right combinations create sustainable flowerbeds, which will also become beautiful from an ornamental point of view.

Combining essences that have the same characteristics and needs is an excellent practice to be rediscovered to create good botanical associations. To meet them, you have to ask yourself the right questions: Do they want wet or dry soil? Do they like acidic or alkaline soils? When do they bloom?

If you want to do the so-called 'companion planting' seriously, you don't need to be an agronomist; a little research can be enough to create botanical partnerships in your garden that are destined to last for years, if not even decades. And you can start with the winning pairs that we suggest here.

Tulip + Peony

The correspondence of amorous senses is almost perfect: they love the sun and well-drained soil and attract precious bees. You can plant them in autumn; the tulip blooms in the first part of spring, the peony in the second, and their flowers touch each other! If you add a summer-flowering gaura, it's ménage a trois and... add spice to a report that has become worn out in the June heat.

Hydrangea + Impatiens + Mint

It is the perfect combination for north-facing terraces: the three plants love the shade and moist soils. The purple of hydrangeas goes well with the pink of impatiens. Mint is beneficial but tends to be intrusive, so it's better to relegate it to a vase: it won't disturb anyone and will continue to keep harmful insects away with its scent.

Iris + Hosta + Hemerocallis

If you have a corner of the garden that only gets sun in the morning, here's a solid trio you won't get rid of so quickly! Irises bloom in spring but give structure all year round; hostas show off their hypnotic heart-shaped leaves and eternal hemerocallis light up dull corners with their colorful summer blooms.

Marigold + Tomatoes + Nasturtium

Marigolds and nasturtium should never be missing in the vegetable garden: they drive away parasites, attract pollinating insects and easily plug any hole, suffocating weeds. Ah, nasturtium leaves and flowers, you can eat them in salads; too bad they die in winter, but they spread easily, and you always find them in different places from where you left them.

Rose + Thyme + Grasses

Her majesty rose's maids-in-waiting can be many. Thyme-like calendula, for example, keeps aphids away. In contrast, ornamental grasses like stipa have the dual function of sheltering the base or climbing ones from the sun and, at the same time, softening the excessive rigidity of many scented roses with large flowers.

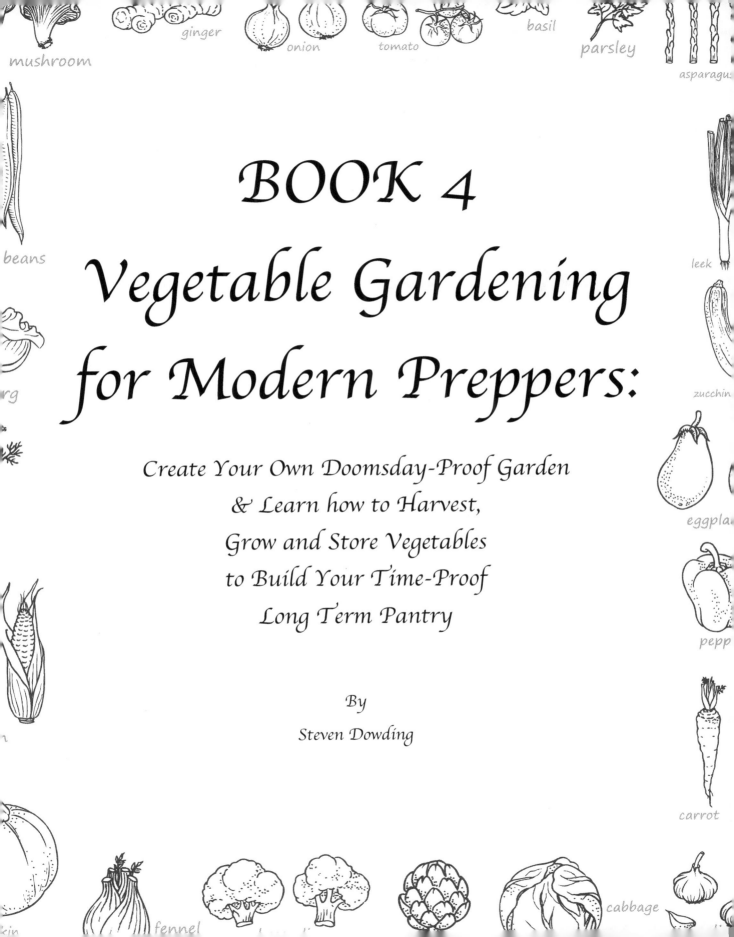

BOOK 4
Vegetable Gardening
for Modern Preppers:

Create Your Own Doomsday-Proof Garden
& Learn how to Harvest,
Grow and Store Vegetables
to Build Your Time-Proof
Long Term Pantry

By

Steven Dowding

Chapter 1.
VEGETABLE GARDEN:
ESSENTIAL FOR MODERN PREPPERS

I t is useless to deny or minimize it: the pandemic has changed our lives and changed us. Since we understand the dangers that humanity could run at any moment, we are no longer the same.

The desire for salvation, preparation, self-sufficiency and the spirit of survival are just some of the words and concepts that have appeared in our daily lives.

Our homes, moreover, are increasingly being designed for self-sufficient living, both for preppers and for enjoying life off the grid. Often relying on alternative energy and advanced security systems, they are located in remote locations because they are not dependent on connection to a community electricity system. They often include ample space for stock storage.

Living in a socially distanced area away from cities and crowds is a trend now, causing unprecedented housing shortages in small towns.

Buyers are more open to unconventionally styled homes with lots of storage for supplies. The prepper lifestyle is widespread, with recent studies estimating more than 20 million preppers worldwide: data also confirmed by Bradley Garrett, the social geographer at University College Dublin.

Garret affirms that there is a sort of insatiable desire for self-reliance and security in this age of uncertainty and that this is culturally and politically different from before. It is strangely one of the few communities we find today that isn't really partisan.

The focus is on learning basic and advanced survival skills, such as water purification techniques, basic medical care, storing and preserving, and how to power electrical devices without access to the mains.

And a fundamental factor, also and above all, being able to feed oneself despite everything, becoming completely self-sufficient concerning mainstream stocks.

Here, then, that building a vegetable garden and raising it professionally and profitably becomes essential for the modern prepper.

Chapter 2.

DOOMSDAY-PROOF SURVIVAL GARDEN: WHAT TO KNOW

It doesn't matter why you start a survival garden: some do it to keep their family well fed, with food one knows where it comes from, others to have autonomy in case of problems. A survival garden is a garden that will it allows you to live mainly on the products you grow. If an emergency or an earthquake affects your community or if an accident prevents you from going to the market, this kind of garden will keep your family fed for a while.

If you want to have a survival garden, planning is key: from what is planted to how it is planted, careful programming will pay off if you need to turn to your survival garden for any reason.

The good news is that, even in good times, your vegetable garden will be a source of tasty natural foods that can lower your monthly food budget. The plus factors important to consider when starting a survival garden are:

- the substances and nutrients you need in order to live well;
- your ability to save seeds so to able to replant your garden;
- the best conservation crops;

- plants that give you the best performance.

What is a Survival Garden?

Survival gardens are more difficult to maintain than a regular garden: if it fails, you have nothing to eat.

You have to think about storage and maximum calories. Also, which plants will provide the most yield tall? It makes no sense to plant vegetables that provide only a small amount of produce that won't keep well. The composition of your survival garden will also depend on other supplies. You may have a vegetable garden, an herb garden, chickens, and cattle, so what you produce will vary from someone who doesn't. It's hard to live by plants alone, so you need to make sure you can count on as many nutrients from the plant as possible in your garden, including fats.

Choosing Your Plants

How much should you grow? The first thing to consider is precisely the answer to this crucial question.

- Ask yourself the following questions:
- How many family members will you feed?
- How much do you currently consume?
- Will you share your harvest with others?

One way to calculate your needs is to monitor what you or your family eat for a month and calculate the calories and quantity. You can also use a calculator online to determine how many calories you need. You might be surprised how much you need to keep yourself and your family healthy.

What Should You Grow?

There are several factors to weigh when deciding what to grow. First of all, consider the growing season and the months when it doesn't grow much in your area. If the growing season is short, you will need plants that keep well, contain the maximum amount of nutrients, and do not require a long season of growth. Of course, you also need to factor in what grows well in your area.

Do you have long winters with few days of sun? Does it snow where you live? If so, you may need a greenhouse to extend the growing season. A heated greenhouse is still better.

Here you can find a list to get you started. These plants generally contain nutrients and grow in most areas:

- Potatoes;
- Corn;

- Jewish;
- Sunflower seeds;
- Tomatoes;
- Beans;
- Pumpkins;
- Onions;
- Beets.

You may be wondering why I listed sunflower seeds. If you live in your garden, you have to get fats in your diet. Sunflowers have a good amount of fat. If they don't grow where you live, go for peanuts!

Also, living from your garden is only possible if you can store a large part of crops to help you during the lean seasons. All of the following plants keep well:

- Onions;
- Beet;
- Turnip;
- Pumpkin;
- Potato;
- Zucchini;
- Garlic;
- Sweet potato;
- Parsnip;
- Winter squash.

To make food last even longer, consider growing what you can ferment, dry, or preserve, such as:

- Cucumbers;
- Peppers;
- Tomatoes;
- Corn;
- Beet;
- Cabbages;
- Jewish;
- Soy;
- Nutrient crops.

Of course, the list of plants growing in your area may differ from the plants above. The key is to try and get different vegetables to ensure you are getting different vital nutrients.

Try to have at least the following:

- Green leafy vegetables for iron;
- Peas, beans, or tubers for carbohydrates;
- Brussels sprouts, lentils, walnuts, or spinach for iron;
- Peppers, berries, tomatoes, kiwis, citrus fruits, or sprouts for vitamin C;
- Asparagus, cucumbers, Brussels sprouts, or beets for vitamins and folic acid.

Saving Seeds

Not only do you have to feed for the first year, but you have to make sure you can plant new crops next year if things keep going badly. After you've considered storage, yield, and nutrition, think about the best plants for storing seeds.

I have always liked vegetables that have many seeds that are easy to harvest. Also, if you have leftover seeds, you can trade them with your neighbors for the stuff you need. The best vegetables for storing seeds are:

- Tomatoes;
- Potatoes;
- Peppers;
- Pumpkins;
- Pumpkins;
- Melons;
- Green peas;
- Jewish;
- Cucumbers;
- Radishes;
- Lettuce.

Seed savings are achieved by using native seeds for planting and by storing vegetable seeds after harvest. Store-bought seeds aren't the best fit, so for your survival garden, you should start with native seeds.

Avoid cross-pollination between plants and study tips and tricks to save seeds. Part of a survival garden's success lies in learning as much as possible from gardeners' experts. Still, we will see better how to do it in Book 6!

How to Prepare the Ground

Other than the plants you plan to grow, choosing a location is the most crucial factor in planning your survival garden. How much space do you need, then?

First, ask yourself: how much space do you need? The amount of garden you need, in fact, depends on your personal circumstances, such as the number of people in your house and the type of plants you are growing.

You also need to take into account if you plan to leave a part of the garden unplanted from time to time. You have to give them rest. Whenever a garden rests, you should provide it with a balanced fertilizer, such as good homemade compost. Calculate the space you need and make sure your garden fits your needs. Even the best vegetables in the world won't survive if they don't reach the amount of sun they need. Choose a location that receives 8 hours of sun a day, perhaps with some shade in the afternoon if you live in a hot area.

I also noticed that there are plants that grow well in the shade (as we saw in the shady vegetable garden in Book 3.)

Preparing the Soil

Eating from the food, you grow in your garden means you must do everything possible to increase the productivity of your garden. The more food you can produce, the better you will be. This means preparing the ground for planting. The healthier your soil, the healthier your plants will be, and the healthier you will be.

The best moment and time to start a survival garden it's when you don't need it. You have to practice and not learn everything in hard times! Save seeds, planting during the four seasons; preserving is something you learn over time.

Try growing something you've never tried before; save seeds from crops

today and to preserve the food you grow.

Challenging Yourself

If you want to see if you've planned your survival garden well, try planting

a garden and feeding your family with it for about a month. Tell the members of your family that you are giving life to a survival garden and that once the harvest begins, no vegetables will be purchased from the store during the process. In this way, you can put test your skills as you buy the rest of the food in the shop or supply it yourself.

This will give you a clear idea of how much effort and work needs to be done in your region and how much you need to farm to replace all vegetables, not to mention the rest of the food.

My last suggestion is to read, learn, and don't be scared to try. The time to learn is now, not when you need a survival garden!

Let's see in detail how to start your Doomsday-Proof Survival Garden!

Chapter 3.
MODERN PREPPER VEGETABLE GARDEN: STEPS AND TECHNIQUES

Creating a vegetable garden is a great idea for everyone and, as we have seen, especially for preppers. In fact, a vegetable garden can offer various benefits, including a certain degree of independence from supermarket supplies, the certainty of eating organic food, and even personal satisfaction.

In fact, a good prepper should aspire to achieve as much independence as possible from the supplies of shops and supermarkets, learning to produce food himself.

Creating a small vegetable garden is not complicated, and it is possible to do it on a small plot of land, in a garden, and even on a balcony.

This Chapter aims to be a guide for those who want to start but don't know. We will see together:

- the basic principles of cultivation
- how to choose the soil and plants.

Where to Build the Garden

If you have a large garden at your disposal, choose the spot with the best exposure to the sun. To have a luxuriant vegetable garden, it is necessary to choose flat land, sheltered from the wind and exposed to the sun (south, south-east, south-west). Avoid basins or depressions in the ground where water stagnation could be created.

If the dimensions allow it, do not create spaces with 'artistic' shapes for the space of your garden, which are then difficult to manage.

Divide it into flower beds by separating them with a length of about 50 cm. The flower beds themselves must not be too large, or you will risk not being able to collect the vegetables in their center without trampling on the area or the vegetables present in it.

Designing it on paper first is a useful technique. While you are doing it, also consider intercropping, i.e., the simultaneous cultivation of different plant species, which are grown side by side, in order to help each other.

Soil

The first step to take is certainly the choice of land where to grow your own plants.

Each soil has different characteristics and may or may not host certain types of vegetables; however, in general, the soil must possess certain characteristics.

The choice of land must be based on the following:

- Exposure to climate and atmospheric agents;
- Conformation of the land - It must not be too stony; it must not have depressions that could cause swamps; it must not have too steep a slope;
- Preparation - Once the land has been chosen, it needs to be prepared so that it can accommodate the vegetables that will be planted. For this, the soil must be worked by tilling it, eliminating weeds, stones, and roots that can prevent the growth of vegetables, then the soil must be fertilized thoroughly.

Choosing Vegetables and Sowing

Once the right soil has been chosen and prepared, it's time for the next phase: sowing.

You can choose to sow or transplant the young seedlings. Sowing directly into the ground can be very risky and requires a certain amount of experience.

For those approaching this activity, it is advisable to buy already formed seedlings and transplant them or sow them in the greenhouse.

So which vegetables to plant and which ones to start with?

For a novice, it is recommended to plant a maximum of 3 or 4 types of vegetables surrounded by aromatic plants and flowers. In fact, biodiversity in a vegetable garden is essential to give the soil all the nutrients that will then be used to create new life.

The choice of vegetable must be made taking into account some elements:

- the climate;
- the type of land;
- the period in which it is decided to sow.

Although practically any type of plant can be planted, the growth of plants that are not suitable for the soil and climate of the place where the garden is being created depends on artificial aids such as herbicides or special fertilizers and a large amount of time and energy to devote. This is explained, of course, because, obviously, an organism that is not suitable for a certain place or climate is more subject to falling ill or struggling to thrive compared to an autochthonous organism that has developed all the necessary defenses over time.

For a neophyte, therefore, it is more suitable to plant native vegetables and, therefore, suitable for the soil and climate of the place.

Furthermore, each vegetable has its own specific sowing and harvesting period.

Plant in Stages Technique

Plant the same vegetable one to two weeks apart.

For example, if you plant a row of lettuce now and another in about ten days, you will not have the lettuce invasion in just one period, but two rows will start producing earlier, and another will prolong the harvest. This mechanism is very useful for vegetables that we cannot preserve in any other way or if we have little time to dedicate ourselves to preservation in oil or preserves.

If you live in an area where evening temperatures are still close to freezing, wait for warmer weather to plant your tomatoes and peppers. Drops in temperature during the growth phase would cause the seedling to suffer or perish.

Cultivation

After preparing the soil and sowing, now is the time for the actual cultivation: the seedlings must be taken care of to grow vigorously!

One of the constant activities is the elimination of weeds. This activity takes a long time but can be eliminated through mulching.

Mulching consists of covering the soil around the vegetables in order to prevent other plants from growing by 'stealing' the nutrients of our seedlings. It is also very useful for maintaining a good level of soil moisture.

Mulching can be done with artificial materials such as sheets or with hay or waste materials such as dry leaves, grass, etc.

Irrigation

Irrigation is the other activity that serves to care for plants. The quantity and frequency depend on the period in which it is being grown, on the characteristics of the soil, and on the characteristics of the vegetables.

For example, if we are in summer, we should constantly use water, especially if it is grown in very draining soil and with plants that need a lot of water.

In any case, there is no mathematical rule for irrigation, just use a little common sense and, above all, experience.

However, some general rules can be established:

- Do not irrigate during the warmest hours of the day to prevent part of the water from evaporating;
- Irrigate with water at room temperature so as not to create a thermal shock;
- Avoid watering the green parts, such as the leaves. Better to prefer irrigation at the base of the plant so as to avoid fungal diseases.

Follow the Phases of the Moon

Depending on the phase of the moon, the vegetables to plant are different.

The basic principle behind this theory is that the waxing moon stimulates the development of the aerial part of the plants, thus favoring foliar vegetation and fruiting.

The waning moon, on the contrary, would reverse the resources of the plant on the root system. We speak of lifebloods that, in the waxing moon, rise towards the surface, while in the waning moon, they descend into the subsoil and then head to the roots.

Growing Vegetables on the Balcony

If you plant on the balcony or terrace, consider the load that can be supported by the floor and the size of the boxes at your disposal.

For short-cycle vegetables (lettuces, salads, aromatic plants), the minimum depth of the earth must be 30 cm.

If you want to plant tomatoes, one of the most popular vegetables, place them in a sunny spot. The vase must have a capacity of at least 60 liters and a good depth (more than 40cm). Some small strains will fit inside a 30cm pot, but the roots will be tight, and your yield may not be very impressive.

If you have limited space for your garden but still want to create your prepper-proof vegetable garden, go straight to the next chapter!

Chapter 4.
SURVIVAL IN POTTED PLANTS

Do you dream of a house overflowing with greenery, capable of providing you with sustenance and love, but you really don't know where to start? Are repotting, mixing the soil, and humidifying as a prepper would do still mysteries for you?

Here's some good news: the basic practices for getting lush and healthy potted plants aren't complicated at all, and once you learn them, they're like riding a bicycle; you never forget them. Let's scroll through the ABC of the green thumb together: plants will become part of your survival!

Dosing Light and Heat

Light is the first ingredient in the recipe for amazing plants. At home, it is necessary to distinguish between winter and summer light: the former is more subdued than the latter. Therefore, those plants which in winter must be brought closer to the window must be moved away in summer to avoid burns.

When the days in the autumn months begin to shorten, it is advisable to move the plants to less than one and a half meters from the windows in order to allow them to take advantage of the few hours of light available. In case they are in poorly lit areas, it can be compensated for with artificial lighting and arranging fluorescent lamps or tubes with a specific color temperature for plant growth.

The same concept, but inversely, for heat sources, such as radiators or stoves. Plants don't like them: before starting the heating, move them to a place where direct heat cannot reach them.

Keep in mind that the presence of dust on the leaves can be an obstacle to the absorption of light; it is, therefore, advisable to periodically clean the leaves with a simple cloth moistened with water, with the exception of plants with hairy leaves in surface, which, on the other hand, should never be wet.

If you see that the plants stretch their stems towards the light and the leaves turn yellow, they are surely suffering from insufficient lighting.

Loam

Preparing the soil specifically for each plant is essential for their health: those that love humidity will do well in a soil mixed with peat, capable of retaining water for longer, while cacti and all plants that they do not like having their roots soaked in water, they will prefer a substrate of soil mixed with sand or inert material such as fine gravel.

Avoid using universal soil as it is: it must always be corrected and modulated according to the specific needs of your plant.

Group Plants

Houseplants love being in company: grouping several plants close together is a clever way of creating a humid microclimate suitable for the plants, exploiting the evaporation of the humidity present in the soil, which will thus be multiplied.

Clean Tools = Fewer Diseases

A healthy plant comes from healthy soil and pot. Having only a small area to live in, the potted plant needs an environment that is as free from pathogens as possible. Here then, is that thorough cleaning of pots and tools becomes indispensable.

Plastic pots can be cleaned with soap and water, while terracotta pots are freed from dirt and salts that have surfaced with a baking soda-based cleaning cream. Wet a handful of baking soda with very little water so as to form a cream, and pass a rough sponge or a brush for vases inside and out; rinse and leave to dry upside down.

When and How to Water

It is always better not to water indoor plants too often since the vast majority of them tolerate dry periods better than too humid ones. Terracotta pots let the roots breathe better even by retaining the water a little longer, a circumstance that allows you to water less often.

In the case of plants with a trunk or large stems, it will be enough to water them about every two weeks; otherwise, once a week. Wait for the soil to be dried before watering again. If, after wetting the plant, you find water in the saucer, this must be eliminated.

How to Humidify

A factor closely related to irrigation, extremely important for the well-being of houseplants, is air humidity. In fact, many of them like a humidity rate that fluctuates between 70% and 90%, which is impossible to maintain inside the home.

The situation can be corrected by placing the plants near a humidifier or by placing expanded clay balls soaked in water in the saucers, the evaporation of which will contribute to the creation of a humid cloud around the plant.

In summer, or in any case, when the temperature remains above 20 degrees, water can instead be vaporized on the leaves with a simple spray.

Move plants outside in the summer (and shelter them in the winter)

Even indoor plants are like an outdoor holiday during the summer. If you have a garden or a balcony, towards the end of May, you can start acclimatizing them outside: first only during the day, then after a week, they can be left day and night.

However, take care not to expose them to direct sun, and monitor the humidity level of the soil more closely.

At the end of summer, also the return must be gradual: first only at night, then withdraw them definitively when the maximum daytime temperatures go under 77 °F (25 °C.)

Feeding the Plants

As for the fertilizer, it can be used in the moments of greatest growth of the plant, i.e., between March and September. It should be chosen according to specific needs: for green plants, flowering plants, orchids, cacti... Always remember to dilute the product, usually liquid, and never use it pure; follow the dilution instructions on the label.

Repotting

When growth is stunted and flowering is poor, it's likely time to report. Better to carry out the operation with a pot about 2-3 cm more in diameter towards the end of winter, before the plant comes out of its rest period. Extract the plant with its loaf of earth from the pot, remove the topsoil and all that falls by gently shaking the block of roots; use a new mixture of soil, reinsert the plant and top up, then water well.

Now that we finally know how to create a prepper vegetable garden at home, especially when we have little space outside, let's find out the mistakes not to make to count on a 'living' prepper pantry 365 days a year.

Chapter 5.
8 MISTAKES PREPPERS CANNOT AFFORD

Cultivation in pots is very rewarding, to the point that even those with large gardens still keep plants in pots. Often, however, the beginnings are a bit 'messy.' Let's try to understand why and what to do to avoid the most common mistakes.

1. Poor Drainage

The number one and most terrible mistake is the one that does not forgive. The drainage must be related to the vase, possibly with large shards at the bottom, to be covered with smaller stones. In really huge pots or tubs, a tightly woven mesh should also be applied between the drainage and the soil, along with a layer of geotextile. Otherwise, the earth would wash away too easily.

Do not use expanded clay but common stones or pumice. Sometimes it is possible that the Authority in your region can provide you with waste material, check and clean it, or give you advice on how to obtain it.

The shards of broken vases and inert material from aquariums (more expensive) are excellent.

2. Wrong Soil

Each plant requires a specific soil. If you want good results, avoid industrial potting soil. Nothing is like the "real earth"! True, it's heavy to carry, but it's worth the effort.

The so-called garden earth (or country soil, collected under the trees, subject to licenses and permits) is unsurpassed. Well-worked with compost and sand, supplemented as needed with mineral fertilizers or manure, it is the basis for good cultivation.

Obviously, the proportions will vary depending on the plant, as well as the type of fertilizer to be mixed when planting.

Too wet soil is sometimes not good: it tends to compact and retain too much water, becoming asphyxiated: you will notice it if it smells like rotten water.

The manure in the pot (as well as the earthworm humus) should be used sparingly and redistributed on the surface in winter. Periodically the plants must be flared, and the soil changed.

3. Too Low or Too High Level

A very common mistake is to get the soil level wrong. Two or three cm from the edge of the vase, and no more, no less. Above all, never less, because the pot would collect too much rainwater, the edge would shade the collar of the plants, and the ventilation would be poor, as well as an evident decrease in the vital space for the roots.

4. Bad Plant Choice, Wrong Ratios, Overcrowding

Sick or stunted plants must be discarded (it is meritorious that you then want to recover them in separate pots).

Pot and plant must be proportionate, the bread of roots must find ample space, and the aerial part must have free space to develop adequately; therefore, do not squeeze the plants like herrings.

5. Too Low or Too High Collar

All plants must have the collar at the same height, which must be that of the soil (not one buried and one half out!). Take this into account when placing the plants, creating enough space for all the earthen bread without compressing it.

6. Irregular Watering

There is nothing worse than giving too much water and then letting the soil dry out. Industrial soils lose their elasticity and ability to absorb water, becoming waterproof. The soil should be moderately moist for plants that love water and dry on the surface for those that need less. But you should never let all the bread dry completely; this would lead to lethal shock.

7. Killer Saucer

The saucers are exclusively functional to respect the condominiums, the neighbors, the civic sense, and the cleanliness of the floor. They must be emptied, always. And where possible, do without them or fill them with pumice or gravel in order to prevent the water from soaking the bottom of the vase. There are also special spacers.

From a horti-cultural point of view, they are useful for hygrophilous or bog garden plants. Other than that, they are excellent trays.

8. Thinking You're Done

Do you think that's all? Growing in pots is convenient but imposes a certain discipline on modern preppers. Learn as much as possible about the plants you grow and try to give them the best conditions (light, water, fertilizers, repotting, etc.). The pots must be followed all year round.

Chapter 6.
STORING VEGETABLES FOR HARD TIMES

Once you've learned how to grow and harvest your own prepper garden veggies, we're left with figuring out how to preserve them for the worst of times. Here are two basic methods.

Vegetables to Keep in the Freezer, Raw

Here is my procedure, which is very simple:

- I spread my dear old newspapers on the table (you can use a tablecloth);
- I provide myself with a chopping board and knife, various bowls, a colander;
- I wash the vegetables well and put them in bowls;
- One by one, I cut the vegetables into small pieces according to the use I have to make of them;
- I dry them well;
- I put them in the freezer in airtight containers with their label.

The idea is to bring out the vegetables on the spot when I need them, having already gotten the job done. It takes less than the traditional meal prep, in which I cook the vegetables (see below), and it doesn't take too long to cook either: just put everything in the pan and sauté for a few minutes to have fresh and crunchy vegetables.

The important thing is to cut the vegetables of the 'right' size, based on the occasions of use, for example:

- sticks, if I have to use them in the oven or quickly sauté them in a pan;
- into small cubes if I have to use them as a sauce for pasta;
- minced, for example, for sautéing;
- into pieces all the same for the minestrone.

Do frozen vegetables lose vitamins? No, frozen vegetables keep their characteristics practically unchanged, as do meat and fish: we can consume them regularly, in the natural version (therefore not those prepared with sauces, gravies, and preservatives).

The Ministry of Health, in the Guidelines for healthy eating, says that frozen vegetables are comparable to fresh ones: so don't worry and start storing!

So we must have a good freezer and learn how to freeze food well since we cannot do industrial freezing at home.

Some use the blast chiller, which cools quickly. Honestly, I've always done without them, and the vegetables we eat always taste great.

Then, honestly: none of us under normal conditions have vitamin deficiencies! In fact, we're all overfed, so we certainly don't lack nutrients; that's it.

Vegetables to Keep in the Freezer, Cooked

If the idea of uncooked frozen foods doesn't appeal to you, you can always opt for traditional meal prep, cooking your veggies.

In this case, here's how I organize myself:

- I put the cooked vegetables in the fridge to be consumed within two days, and stored in airtight containers;
- I put the other cooked vegetables in the freezer, which I take out when I need them.

I usually prefer simple cooking: steam, pressure, oven. Sometimes I cook in a pan if it's hot, but usually – as soon as the temperatures permit, I cook everything in the oven.

My equipment for organized meal prepping:

- airtight containers of various shapes;
- paper tape and an indelible marker to mark all the containers by writing the contents and the date of preparation;
- very simple and super cheap steamer: I cook the vegetables already in small pieces, and I make them go full circle;

- instant pot: my latest purchase, which allows me to cook pressure, steam, slow, and a thousand other types, which I use for cooking dried vegetables;
- very basic low trays: I really like them, and I use them in a continuous stream;
- silicone baking mats: to eliminate disposable baking paper.

It's about changing your mindset: meal prepping is a choice dictated by limited time and the need to eat 'healthy' things, especially if they come from your garden.

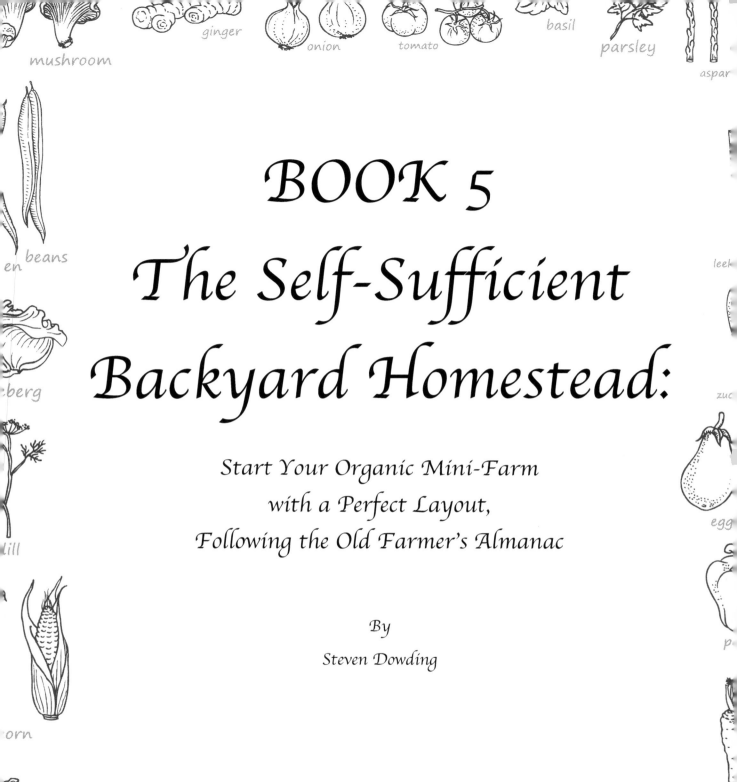

BOOK 5
The Self-Sufficient
Backyard Homestead:

Start Your Organic Mini-Farm
with a Perfect Layout,
Following the Old Farmer's Almanac

By

Steven Dowding

Chapter 1.
LIKE ANCIENT FARMERS DID

In the previous books, we have learned the history of vegetable gardens, we have seen what the main steps to do it, especially with a pest-free approach are, discovered the many types of cultivation you have available for your garden, and, finally, how to create one suitable for preppers.

In this book, finally, we are going to analyze even more in detail how to start your self-sufficient backyard homestead, an organic mini-farm with a perfect layout following the Old Farmer's Almanac.

What's the Old Farmer's Almanac? It's a very vital tool for setting up your mini-farm so that it is linked to natural cycles, sustainable and prosperous.

This Almanac, on the other hand, began publication in 1792. As the oldest published periodical in North American history, it started a few years after a fateful summer when farmers suffered and were unable to produce a large crop that was due to the weather. For this very reason, The Old Farmers' Almanac is now famous for its ability to predict the weather and the harvest over long periods of time.

The book includes astronomical dates and also incorporates trivia and humor. It adds simple tips on things like fishing, cooking, and gardening, promoting healthy living, conservation, and simple core values in every issue.

Moreover, the Farmer's Almanac includes various recipes and predicts technology and trends in fashion and home decor.

Weather forecasts are supposed to be made using a secret formula that has been passed down over the years but never said to anyone. Not only is the formula kept secret, but so is the weatherman. The secret formula is used in conjunction with several scientific calculations of various solar activities. Past weather records are analyzed, and specific weather patterns are detected and identified.

The Farmers' Almanac is annually published in Maine through the Almanac Publishing Company on the second Tuesday of September and is dated for the following year. The Almanac Publishing Company certifies that the predictions within The Farmers' Almanac have an accuracy of 80-85% of being true. However, scientists disagree with those claims and have argued that their predictions are no better than anything left to chance. Forecasters sometimes refer to The Farmers' Almanac, comparing it to the current weather for amusement.

Controversy aside, however, many people use this Almanac to see what the weather forecast is and rely on it, basing their decisions on vacations, growing vegetables, or other plans for the coming year.

In addition to the American version, there is also a Canadian version. Over the years, The Farmer's Almanac has gained national publicity, and various publishers have continued the legacy by keeping it on shelves around the world.

We'll use it to evaluate how to build a self-sufficient backyard homestead following natural, sustainable and reliable rhythms all year round... just like ancient farmers did!

Chapter 2.
THE ANSWER IS HOMESTEADING

Modern life is full of 'comfortable' things for one's sustenance; however, more and more people prefer a simpler, more self-sufficient lifestyle. The farm lifestyle offers ways for people to create their own energy, conserve resources, grow their own food, and raise animals for milk, meat, and honey.

Life on a mini-farm is just a classic example. While this lifestyle may not be right for everyone, some of the simpler practices can also be used in urban settings.

What is homesteading, then? Build a space around your home (usually a back garden) that becomes completely self-sufficient. Usually, we think of someone who lives outside of society's food and energy chains. Talking over the years with some of my neighbors about homesteading, I realized that the central objective is precisely self-sufficiency, which can even involve avoiding the use of money, replaced by bartering to obtain the necessary goods. In summary, therefore, it means doing what you can for yourself in the space where you live.

Homesteading was a pioneering term that meant that you were given government land to use and develop. This is how the regions became established and contributed much of the spread throughout North America. During the beatnik and hippy era, the term made a comeback as disillusioned young people – often preppers or seed savers – shaped a new personalized lifestyle away from the cities.

The farm lifestyle has flourished again due to conservation concerns, questions about our food supply, the high cost of urban living, and the scarcity of good housing in modern metropolis centers. It's also part of the DIY movement, embraced for its fun way of catering to one's interests.

The most extreme example of this concept is precisely giving life not only to a vegetable garden but to a real farm, where you can grow fruit and vegetables, honey and preserves, raise animals for food, generate your energy with solar panels, and much more.

Such an intense farm may also include hunting and fishing, foraging, making clothes, raising honey bees, and other methods of providing for the family. It also usually includes sustainable agriculture practices and the conservation of resources such as water.

The ultimate goal is to have anything you need at your fingertips: just get organized, engage, work and collect.

Homesteading in Urban Environments

Even a busy citizen can enjoy homesteading. Driving to a U-pick farm in the countryside or keeping your own chickens is quite common.

You can also plant a small garden, keep bees, encourage beneficial insects, compost, pick seasonal mushrooms, and more. Even an apartment building dweller can compost their kitchen scraps with a little vermicompost on their patio or porch.

Being aware of choices and respecting nature are two main homesteading practices. Doing as much as possible for yourself is key to family living in any area.

Let's see together what the steps are to realize this dream of self-sufficiency and environmental sustainability following natural rhythms and the Old Farmer's Almanac.

Chapter 3.
YOUR SELF-SUFFICIENT MINI-FARM

Creating a self-sufficient farm isn't just about growing acres of grain or running a herd of hundreds of cows. Starting a farm is no small feat. You have to consider many things and calculate many variables. However, the idea of creating this new reality is gaining momentum. There are more and more projects whose goal is resilience and this is only a good thing compared to the need to prepare for future changes, from the economic crisis to the environmental, water, energy, and food crisis.

On a Human Scale

On a self-sufficient farm, high-quality food is grown both for the family and for the local community, in an ecological, sustainable way and without the use of fossil fuels which, in addition to damaging the planet, are dangerous for human health. This is the basic concept, which for years has guided all those who have moved towards the creation of self-sufficient farms.

The most developed in America are independent family micro-farms. An economic and sustainable solution that seeks social forms of co-participation and co-responsibility to base its departure. Indeed, it is common among those who undertake this journey to implement crowdfunding campaigns and also to tell and share their personal experience with an ever-growing number of people. In this way, awareness of the quality of life in nature is created, thanks to the rediscovery of the countryside.

Before anything else, it is good to define a work plan relating to both the short and long term. Considering opportunities and impediments and calculating financial and market objectives, as well as personal ones, are tedious activities but fundamental to the success of this project. Once the farm has been chosen, it is necessary to inspect it, examine its land and identify its weak points. Furthermore, drawing an ideal map of the farm that you want to obtain within ten years is an operation that accurately outlines which path you want to take. If you want to create a farm to cultivate, you will also need to have the necessary machinery to sow, tend the crops, till, and harvest. While if the farm is intended for cattle breeding, it is of primary importance to think about fences, management areas, and water systems and to feed them.

Fundamental Aspects

When one thinks of self-reliance, the concepts of freedom and happiness come to mind. Self-sufficiency is something that will never be achieved 100%, but it is a tendency, an attempt to get ever closer to the creation of an alternative and sustainable system.

On farms, being self-sufficient means, for example, consuming water only from springs.

Instead, heating is entrusted to boilers and stoves that burn wood, and hot sanitary water is obtained thanks to solar panels.

Electricity comes from the photovoltaic system, and all the structures that make up the self-sufficient farm have low energy consumption.

The creation of a community and the cooperation of animals are fundamental elements for achieving the goal of self-sufficiency, aspects in which it is necessary to invest in the coming years.

Tips Before Starting

- It takes time and patience: moving into a property is both exciting and a little intimidating. Most people look forward to working the land and seeing things grow. But remember that a farm takes time to grow. There will be trial and error and even some total failures along the way. Learning what you did wrong, as well as the characteristics of your specific land, is an integral part of farming. You may have an end goal to feed your family only with produce from your own property, but understand that it can take years to get to this point.
- Don't underestimate protection: good fences make good neighbors and good farms. Animals should be confined, and predators should be kept away. Fencing may not seem

like a big deal when touring properties, and it can be costly to build new fencing. Look for property listings that mention fencing and double fencing, so you don't incur additional costs after the purchase.

- Make every square foot count: A farmhouse doesn't have to be large; it just needs to be practical. It means using your land to its fullest potential. The same goes for larger lands. Making your land work for you instead of working for it is an essential part of family ownership. Planting a rain garden in a damp part of the property will help take advantage of space that would otherwise be bare. Establish the lawn and mow it only where you and your family actually use and enjoy it. Changing the grass in a pasture or garden is a perfect way to cut down on mowing time and enjoy every patch of your property. We also need to remind new settlers that your lot area isn't completely horizontal. Modern-day growers understand that vertical space above their land is also very useful. Vertical gardens are a natural addition, and you can create layers of growth in a small amount of space. A large amount of food can grow from the trellises, which help make every inch of land productive.

- Know Your Neighbors: Being self-sufficient doesn't mean working alone. There's a reason why cooperative farming is so popular. Families that develop good relationships with neighbors are more successful. Good neighbors pay attention to one another and lend a helping hand when needed. You will also have crops that excel and others that fail. Trading your excess eggs for your neighbors' excess tomatoes can help you get through the tough years. You don't have to grow everything if the community can develop a barter system.

- Your family first: building a home is one of the most rewarding ways to support your family. Not only will you learn more about the land, but you'll also spend quality time with your family as you work towards food independence together. It's a lot of work, but the farm is a meaningful way to make sure you can support your family no matter what.

Basic Farm Activities to Know and Implement

- Self-produce instead of buying
- Reduce waste
- Recycle as much as possible
- Grow your own food (we've seen this in previous books)
- Raise chickens
- Raise bees
- DIY at home
- Repair objects (and don't throw them away)
- Make preserves at home
- Dehydrate/freeze surplus fruits, vegetables, and herbs (we covered this in Book 4)
- Produce candles at home
- Make homemade soap

- Prepare the cheese and bread
- Work the wood
- Learn sewing and techniques such as crocheting, knitting, etc.
- Generate energy with wind or solar panels
- Collect rainwater
- Recycle food waste and compost
- Trade goods and time with neighbors

Start a little at a time, also considering that each choice will have an impact on your lifestyle, your family, your future, and even your economy.

Finally, consider how far you are willing to go.

And prepare a pen and paper to make a list of what you will need starting from the next Chapter!

Chapter 4.
HOW MANY WAYS TO HOMESTEADING?

As mentioned earlier, the homesteading business is not limited to large countryside sustenance. There are many types of homesteading. Let's find out.

The Homestead Apartment

Let's start with the former, considering you're one of the many unfortunate twenty-first-century denizens who are losing out on large tracts of land to live on even though you'd absolutely love to have a sprawling space in which to breathe freely.

An apartment farm isn't as bad as it sounds. There are many things you can grow, nurture, and even marry into something that basically provides you with enough square feet to cover with tile.

If homesteading is all about self-sufficiency, it means being smarter about some things to save some money or have healthier produce to eat.

Potted Gardening

A containerized indoor herb garden is a great way to come home.

Even if there isn't enough space in an apartment, you can take care of some plants in pots and containers. That can save you from the annoyance of tilling the land, and there can be enough produce to support a single person or a household. You can better control the weather in small greenhouses, and plants aren't restricted to certain seasons.

Herb Gardening

We spend a lot of money on essential herbs for our daily cooking. How would you like to save money growing your herbs? They do not ask for much space and can be placed in any window. Every day you will be pampered by the wonderful scent of fresh herbs.

Hydroponic Gardening

You can try the hydroponic gardening system, as it is cleaner, requires no soil, is more efficient, saves resources much more than potting, and also increases the growth rate of plants by many folds.

Poultry Farming

Breeding in the apartment? It seems absurd and impossible unless you can use a Harry Potter spell that creates enough space and amenities.

But it is entirely possible. It is not possible for goats, cows, and the like. But the breeding of small animals is still possible.

Chickens are a popular option to raise for their proficient egg production. If you are looking for meat alternatives or more exotic omelets, quail and duck can be good choices.

Fish Farm

Another option is small-scale urban fish farms. While this isn't ideal, it's just how life on a farm works. Urban fish farming offers many advantages. Firstly, you don't have to spend much on buying fish from the market to cook. Fish can be expensive to consume if you are a seafood lover.

You can also run your own fish farming business from your home and make a lot of money. You'll need to invest a bit in the aquaponic system, which it's not expensive.

Goats and Rabbits

If you want to go beyond fish and poultry but don't mind large mammals, rabbits are a solid option.

Another one is raising pygmy goats. These goats are small enough to fit in your apartment.

They also provide meat and milk, which you might not find in the supermarket.

Preservation

Homesteading isn't just about growing. Storage is also a smart way to conserve resources. You can buy supplies in bulk from a local grocery during sale days and store them for later.

But conservation also complements pot gardening. The fish farm is also covered. Your products can be stored in a can or frozen for later consumption.

You can also visit farms to buy crops directly from the farmer. This eliminates the option of intermediaries, thus paying a fairer price and also helping the farmers. You can buy crops that you know you can grow and save them for later.

Community Gardening

When we can't do something ourselves, it doesn't mean we can't do it at all. Even if you don't feel like staying at home with your family, even if it seems impossible, you can still do it with other people in your community.

The indoor community garden is becoming more popular every year. You will be able to reduce your workload and reap the rewards of your investment while harvesting.

Pantry Making And Cooking

There is no need to spend a lot on kitchen supplies. Instead, you can create your own. All you need are the basic ingredients. By stocking up on pantry supplies and buying them in bulk, you can make everything from buttermilk to sugar syrup cookies.

Similar to stocking up on food, cooking all of your meals at home is a smart decision. This is especially true in Asian homes. Save a lot on your expenses, free your food from preservatives and risk being stale; it smells fresh and is healthier.

You can experiment with the recipes and not be limited to the standard.

Urban Settlement

Urban Homesteading is not a separate category. It is more of an extension of apartment Homesteading. Urban development, on the other hand, is for suburban homeowners who have less than a quarter of an acre. Building an apartment has its challenges.

Urban Farming allows you to grow your farm to greater levels, increase your fish farming, and even add Dexter cattle to your breeding plans.

Dexter cattle are something like pygmy goats but with much more milk-producing ability.

A larger plot of land can make it easier to build a greenhouse or hydroponic system. You can grow more plants with a well-built hydroponic system spread over a large area of land.

Small And Big Traditional Farmhouse

Traditional homesteading is more than a hobby and requires you to seriously consider and reconsider what you are investing in, both physically and monetarily. The bigger the scale, the more difficult it is to manage. With a traditional farm, you spend many hours and work to keep your consumption organic.

But it's not that difficult. There are two options for traditional homesteading: small and large.

You will need at least one acre and an average of two acres to start with the smallest one. In a couple of acres, you can venture into fruit growing, farming, fish farming, and animal husbandry all at the same time. Vineyards, orchards, a couple of greenhouses, and a small crop field seem feasible. You need to keep in mind that homesteading in the traditional way has needs that are sensitive to weather conditions. For the animals, you'll need to either grow enough forage to store it for the winter or purchase it from farmers to save on expenses. You will need a diary and calendar to keep track of all household activities on a daily basis.

A large farm eliminates the need for dependency as you can grow it enough to help maintain stock for your livestock throughout the year, including large cattle, because that becomes totally possible in this scenario. From vegetables and fruit, booze and milk to meat and poultry, a large farm offers enough space for everyone.

So Many Questions

You need to be as open as possible if you want to homestead to be successful, be it urban or rural, small or large. Proactivity is the key to homesteading. Passivity not only makes you feel discouraged, but it also hinders your ability to manage time.

Keeping both a mental and physical checklist is important for homesteading. Think like a researcher in a lab, not a hobbyist. You have to take each step carefully.

Start by growing a couple of herbs. While it sounds simple, once you're proficient at growing herbs to a fresh, healthy, edible state, you'll be able to move on to more complex tasks. Homesteading is easier than ever with plants. Even if the plants die, they don't cause you pain or guilt.

Homesteading is the opposite of monotonous and mundane industrial work. Nourish living beings through family settlement, which is similar to motherhood. It brings out a different kind of feeling.

Be proactive and active. Contribute to the environment and farm of your choice, whether it's in your backyard or in your apartment.

Chapter 5.
STEP-BY-STEP GUIDE

As promised, here is the step-by-step guide to building your mini-farm with an eye on the perfect layout, using the advice of old farmers.

1. Your Project First

Having a work plan before you start is best. Make sure you have reviewed and written down everything in your favor against opportunities and impediments (a so-called 'macro analysis). Consider where you have arrived, where you want to go, and how to do it. It also calculates financial and market goals as well as personal ones.

Before you dive in and start the whole thing, inspect the farm you want to buy by examining the land and every weak point in it, the positive aspects, and areas for improvement. Jot down a map of the whole farm and the various locations. If you want, you can draw another similar but ideal farm, the farm you want to have within ten years of starting it.

2. Evaluate Climate and Terrain

Soil is the 'base' of what, how, and where you will grow or breed.

Look for topographic features, relief, and soil composition.

Study it or test it to see if it's better for growing or breeding.

Look for any native plants around, especially grasses, if you intend to raise livestock.

Talk to other factors besides the one who will sell you everything (if you buy instead of inheriting) to understand what kind of crop yields better (if any are possible), where and when to sow, and when to harvest. If the area is used for grazing, have a forage analysis done together with a soil test.

Go to the municipal or county office in charge and look for information on the different climatic conditions of recent years that have occurred in the area where the farm is located.

Only do this if you are unfamiliar with the area and before or after talking to the seller and any neighbors.

3. Capitalize

If the farm you buy doesn't have any existing buildings, you'll need to have them erected to turn them into your ideal farm. Sometimes many of the existing ones just need to be repaired, and others demolished because they are ruins or too old.

If you create a farm to cultivate, you will also need to have the necessary machinery to sow, tend the crops, till, and harvest.

On the other hand, if you buy a farm to raise livestock and continue with the one you already have, you will have to look after it, the fences, management areas, water, and feed facilities. There are chances of having to change the structures of the existing fences, renew the pastures and create a more suitable habitat for the animals that have degraded it over time and neglect.

4. Choose the Sector you Like

Basically, there are two broad categories of agricultural work that you can choose from: crops, such as cereals (oilseeds, cereals, and legumes), orchards, cultivation of berries and vineyards, production of vegetables, production of hay and forage; and livestock, such as beef or dairy cattle, pigs, poultry, horses, sheep, goats, beekeeping, and even exotic animals. A relatively new and specific sector is that of organic agriculture, which can refer to all agricultural production, as well as livestock breeding, but involves the use of unconventional means.

Commercial/industrial farms usually rely on more than one sector to have a complete farm. For example, a dairy farm cannot be profitable enough if it does not also have a silage, hay, and grain business.

A farm that is dedicated solely to the cultivation of the fields often has to set up a crop rotation program and cultivate at least two different types of product for each season, provide for the rotation of cereals, oilseeds, and/or legumes each year, in order to satisfy the demands of the specific market. Usually, the bigger the farm, the less the need to differentiate production in different sectors, even if this is not always the case; in any case, it is not an aspect to worry about when you have to choose how and where to start your business. You have every right to choose how many sectors and activities you want for your farm.

Many family farms or those managed by a single farmer, regardless of size, often cater to at least five or even more industries. Those farms, even family ones, which are defined as 'mixed,' that is, they deal with both cultivation and livestock, are not so rare.

5. Talk to Expert Farmers

Contact those companies that mainly deal with the sector you are most interested in.

Check if there is any reality of this type in your area that you can visit.

Do an Internet search to find farms or agricultural fairs in your area that you can go to and study. You may meet serious and active farmers to talk to about agriculture and get information from.

You can ask the other farmers what type of crops they deal with, how their activities or the company itself have changed over time, if they have ideas about the most important sector of the moment, in which it is worth investing, and also if you can stop in their farm for a while to visit it well. Farmers are usually friendly, humble, and welcoming people, although some are more cautious and circumspect than others.

Farm fairs and markets are also perfect places to meet other farmers, especially those who specialize in particular sectors (like goat cheese, berries, etc.).

6. Raise Cattle

Determine the area where you want to raise cattle for the next 10, 30, or more years

You need to find a place you know or really like and be sure you can raise animals there.

The place can be anywhere from Canada to South America. Factors such as climate, seasons, markets, vegetation, and topography differ depending on the location you choose.

Choose the type of cattle you want to raise based on your budget and goals. The most common choices are dairy farms or beef farms. Keep in mind that starting a dairy farm is much more expensive and time-consuming. You will also need more equipment to comply with government regulations.

Research the various breeds you can or want to raise. Determine breed type based on the purpose of your farm or ranch, not what you like about it.

Start with a breed that is known for its good temperament and doesn't require too much work. Hereford, Red Poll, Shorthorn, Galloway, and British White are breeds known for their docility.

If you are determined to breed Angus cattle because they are the most popular in your area, please choose the animals very carefully.

If you want to care for dairy cows, the best and most well-known breeds are Holstein, Jersey, and Brown Swiss. Guernsey and Ayrshire may be for you if you are not in North America.

7. Get Prepared: Right Equipment

Research and purchase the type of facilities, equipment, and machinery needed for the type of cattle you have decided to raise

Analyze your business and financial situation to see what you need (not what you want). Fences, water features, and feeders are the priority. A tractor, hay equipment, trailer, and other tools or structures are also important.

If you decide to raise dairy cows, you will need different structures and a milking space, as well as a farrowing facility, a barn for the calves, and a barn to keep the cows when they are not being milked.

If you've decided to raise cattle for sale, fences, some stables, and water sources are probably all you need. Costs will be higher to feed cattle during the winter and if you plan to add grain to their diet.

8. Consider the Lunar Calendar

The work of the horticulturist is deeply linked to the seasons, so it is very important to keep an eye on the calendar, on which the moments of sowing, harvesting, and, consequently, all the other work necessary for cultivation depend. It may therefore be useful to make a month-by-month summary of what is harvested, what is sown, and what work to do in the garden in each season.

Those who want to follow the indications of Old Farmers' traditions can also follow the lunar phases to decide on sowing and transplanting.

To quickly establish what to sow, you can also use a sowing calculator, which, starting from the month and other characteristics, tells you what you can grow in your home garden, also calculating crop rotation.

9. Take Notes

Keep books, parts information, health/vaccines, purchases/sales, etc., in order. The most important books are the financial ones because they allow you to understand if you are at a loss or if you are gaining. Even if the one you are running is a mini-farm.

BONUS: Pieces of Advice

Always expect the unexpected. You never know what might happen as soon as you kick things off.

If you need help or advice, don't be afraid to ask.

Don't take things for granted. Always keep in mind the environment, what you do and how you feel.

Start with one activity at a time and slowly. If you want to avoid debt and bankruptcy, don't go into high gear. Let five or ten years go by. If you have a lot of lands, you could lease it for the first five years until the rest goes to the regime you want.

Don't buy the latest generation machinery. It's a good way to stay broke right away. There are many cars that can be found at auctions for very little compared to their starting value, depending on who is bidding on them and how many people want them.

Know the market, whether it's grain or poultry. Learn when to sell and buy, from whom, and to whom.

Budget before you start and think about a loan to start the farm.

Be very careful of Murphy's Law: If something can go wrong, it will go wrong.

Pro Note: Warnings

Sticking to a budget is a good way to avoid going over upfront costs.

You will have little profit at first. Minimize costs, and you won't go into the red.

Don't put too much meat on the fire. You could get tired or dejected or get in serious trouble with the bank for your lack of discrimination.

Chapter 6.
365-DAYS OLD FARMER'S CALENDAR

Sow Calendar

One crucial thing to do to have a good vegetable garden is to choose the right time to sow.

I advise you to look at the sowing calendar a little in advance in the planning phase. Both because it is necessary to procure the seeds and because it is good to prepare the soil first.

Some crops prefer processing a few months before, while others need to be fertilized, so it's better to do things in time. I, therefore, hope that our sowing calendar will help you plan your garden and your mini-farm activities!

Winter Sowing

Winter is a difficult period for sowing; between December and February, we have the soil, which is often frozen and climatic conditions that are not very suitable for the germination and survival of the garden seedlings. Nonetheless, there is no shortage of work that can be done: working in a hotbed seedbed, the seedlings can be planted in pots, preparing them for spring transplanting. There are also crops that survive with even minimal protection: for example, building a cold tunnel is a way to have fresh vegetables even in winter. Also, in winter, garlic and onions are planted, which bravely face the frozen vegetable garden.

Spring Sowing

Spring is a fundamental period for sowing: once the winter frosts have passed, these are the months in which it is finally possible to sow in the open field and transplant the seedlings into the plots. In the months of March, April and May, there is, therefore, a lot of work for the horticulturist, and there are many vegetables that can be sown. In spring, a large part of the work of the whole calendar year is played out in the garden: if the plants are planted at the right time, the summer and autumn harvest will be rich.

Summer Sowing

With the arrival of summer, sowing continues in the garden, preparing winter and autumn vegetables. Even if you sweat like hell working in the heat, if we want to have fresh vegetables all year round, we have to roll up our sleeves even in August and keep an eye on the summer sowing calendar. After germination, it is essential to be careful because the strong sun and intense heat can put the newborn seedlings in difficulty, as well as any dryness.

Autumn Sowing

Once the summer heat has passed, we move on to sowing those plants that do not fear the first frosts of winter, such as cabbage or cut salads which, having a short cycle, can be harvested in late autumn before the climate becomes too harsh.

Plan plantings based on the desired crop

The harvest period also depends on the sowing period, so we recommend sowing while also taking into account your family's consumption expectations if you want to have a home garden that produces fresh vegetables in order to bring them to the kitchen at the right time.

For an efficient vegetable garden project, it is useful to know both the sowing times and the seasonality of the vegetables.

The scalar sowing method consists in spreading the sowing times over a large period in order to have a more gradual and prolonged harvest; it is a very useful shrewdness in the home garden.

To prolong or anticipate sowing, non-woven fabric covering, greenhouses, and heated seedbeds can be used, thus extending the periods useful for sowing.

Month by Month

January: Also, in winter, the seedbed is organized. Here are which vegetables are planted in January:

February: The hot seedbed is fully operational, while we put broad beans and garlic in the field.

March: Planting potatoes, spring begins, and sowing in the field.

April: Lots of seeds, April is the most important month to do it.

May: Still sowing and many transplants to do; summer is coming.

June: Among leeks, cabbage and courgettes, let's find out what to sow this month.

July: Among the summer sowings, we find fennel, chicory, and turnip greens.

August: The hottest month, between fennel and salads and the first sowing of onions.

September: Winter vegetables are sown in September: the month of cabbages and salads.

October: Winter is approaching, and we sow peas, garlic, onions, and early salads.

November: broad beans, peas, garlic, and onions are planted in the field; the rest are sown in tunnels.

December: There is little to sow in the garden, but garlic, peas, and broad beans defy the frost.

Activities Calendar

The work to be done in the garden changes from season to season: at the end of autumn, the soil is prepared, and the fertilizer is spread; in January, we dedicate ourselves to maintaining the tools and working in the seedbed while the ground is frozen, in spring the bulk of the sowing, in June we take care of weeds, and in the summer we are careful to guarantee correct irrigation.

Knowing when to do the various operations necessary to manage the mini-farm is essential.

An organic garden and a farm require constant attention and dedication that pays off with great satisfaction and excellent healthy vegetables.

Here you will find a month-by-month list of what there is to do in the family garden, inviting all of you workers to roll up your sleeves.

There are many precautions necessary to make a good vegetable garden; here are some of the primary operations to do during the year, with the indicative period in which they are implemented.

- Between December and February: Garden design - Before starting work, it is good to have a plan in the garden as in all things. A little planning means being able to program the crops and make the most of the plots, taking into account the proper crop rotation and useful intercropping. Planning is a task for winter.
- October, November, and March: Soil tillage - Before sowing, it is necessary to dig and prepare the seedbed; it is the preparation of the soil. This work is often done in the garden; it is particularly typical of the months of October, November, and March.
- September - January: Fertilization - The fertilizer can be given all year round, but generally, between autumn and the end of winter, good annual fertilization is done, burying compost or mature manure.
- Between March and May: Seeding and transplanting. To find out the right time to sow and transplant in the garden, it is advisable to consult the respective calendars; this is

obviously a real job, which has its peak between March and May.

- February - July: purchase of farm animals - The best period for the purchase is from February to July so that the birth and breeding of animals take place during the summer. Poultry can be purchased at different ages.

- March - June: Creation of supports for climbing plants - Many plants need guardians to grow properly. Therefore it is necessary to prepare adequate support, a job to be done after sowing or transplanting between spring and early summer.

- May and June: Prunings - Pruning is typical of the orchard, but also, in the vegetable garden, one finds oneself trimming or pruning some crops, for example, tomatoes and pumpkins. Generally, they are duties in the months of May and June.

- Spring: Adversity control. Insects and diseases must be kept under control, monitoring the organic garden and intervening promptly when needed. The most intense months for insect control are spring because it is helpful to intercept the first generation of parasites. For diseases, on the other hand, the rainy periods of autumn and especially spring is the peak of the risk.

- Summer: Irrigation. Wetting the garden is a typical summer job and is very important to ensure a good harvest and plant health.

- June- November: Weed control. Weeds hold court between summer and early autumn, and one of the most tedious jobs is keeping them at bay.

- Protection from cold and atmospheric agents. To avoid frosts, hailstorms, or too much sun, depending on the season, it is necessary to take steps to protect horticultural plants.

- Late Spring / Late Summer: Honey Harvest - Honey is harvested about two times a year, after the spring and the summer harvest.

- All Year (Mostly Summer): Harvesting - Among the most pleasant jobs is collecting the result of cultivation; you need to know how to do it at the right time and in the right way to take well-ripened vegetables. A well-managed family garden offers a year-round harvest, but summer is undoubtedly the wealthiest time.

- November and December: Maintenance - There are many small maintenance jobs, tools, and structures related to the garden, this type of activity is excellent for downtime, for example, in the months of November and December.

Harvest Calendar

To plan the harvest correctly, you need to know two things:

- The sowing calendar, i.e., when it is possible to sow each vegetable;
- The duration of the crop cycle of the desired vegetables, i.e., how long the plant takes on average from sowing to harvest. The second figure depends a lot on the variety sown; it can be found indicated on the seed sachets.

For a family garden, it is very useful to sow in stages, i.e., not sow a single type of vegetable en masse but stagger the sowing operations as much as possible. In this way, the harvest will also be gradual, and the period in which all types of vegetables are available will be extended.

Let's see for each month which vegetables are in season and what can be harvested in the garden.

January and February Vegetables

In January, various winter vegetables can be harvested in the garden: chard, beetroot, many salads (such as Catalonia, endive, radicchio, rocket), practically all cabbages (cauliflower, kohlrabi, cabbage, broccoli, Brussels sprouts, savoy cabbage), fennel, celeriac, parsnips, spinach, radishes, carrots, turnip tops, salsify and salsify, leeks, pumpkin. Then there are various aromatic herbs such as rosemary, sage, and thyme whose harvest extends for almost the whole year.

March Vegetables

In March, winter vegetables such as cabbage, parsnips, fennel, leeks, and a few more pumpkins are still harvested. Continue spinach, turnip tops, carrots, radishes, the various salads in protected cultivation, and the aforementioned aromatics. Add onions, garlic, beets, artichokes, and potatoes.

April Harvest

April is a transitional month in our harvest calendar: we find the last winter vegetables in the garden (fennel, leeks, and cabbage), we continue with artichokes, garlic, and onions, and with all those crops that are sown in stages and that do well in tunnels: rocket, head and cutting lettuce, carrots, radishes, parsley. Then the first spring vegetables, such as peas, arrive, and ribs and rhubarb also begin to appear.

May, June, and July Harvest

In these months, the production of the garden comes alive, and we have most of the vegetables available that ripen between spring and summer.

Great variety, therefore, in the garden and on the table: we can harvest garlic, onions, carrots, radishes, chard, rocket, radicchio, lettuce, spinach, peas, asparagus, potatoes, and parsley.

We begin to find the first aubergines, tomatoes, green beans, courgettes, and cucumbers. Peppers, beans, and pumpkins are added with the arrival of summer.

There will then be almost all the aromatic herbs available, from chives to sage, passing through the mint, thyme, rosemary, and sage. If we have an orchard or if we have grown small fruits, they will give us satisfaction in these months.

August and September Vegetables

August is another very rich month for the garden, like July, in which the horticulturist reaps the fruits of his hard spring work. In the garden, we find watermelons, beets, celery, pumpkins and zucchini, broccoli, cucumbers, peppers, hot peppers, tomatoes, aubergines, beans, potatoes, and onions.

The month of September is a bridge between summer and autumn, so we still find summer varieties, especially chilies, tomatoes, and courgettes. It is also the ideal month for aromatic herbs: especially those such as basil must be harvested, which then closes the crop cycle. Ready to cook a good Genoese pesto?

October Harvest

October in the harvest calendar sees the beginning of autumn vegetables: thistles and fennel are ready to be picked, and courgettes, pumpkins, and cucumbers continue. We find the last peppers and aubergines in the garden, and there are also cruciferous vegetables (the various cabbages and cauliflowers), some salads (lettuce, rocket, lamb's lettuce), carrots, spinach, and radishes.

November and December Vegetables

November and December are the months with the least variety. However, there are several winter vegetables that we can harvest in these cold months. We can also help by protecting the crops with cold sheets or tunnels: we find carrots, radishes, lettuce, spinach, turnips, chicory, and various species of cabbage in the garden, all resistant vegetables that do not fear winter.

The indications on the harvesting of vegetables are to verify as the climatic conditions and the sowing period influence and can vary the ripening of the vegetables.

The Old Farmer's Almanac should therefore be kept as a guideline: it's up to every farmer, then, to understand when the vegetables should be harvested, looking at how their plants are doing.

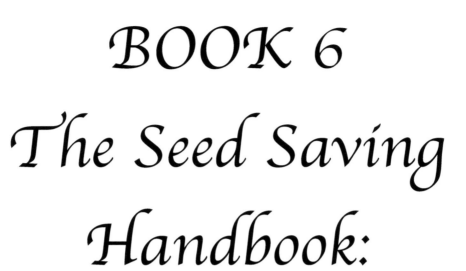

BOOK 6
The Seed Saving Handbook:

Harvest, Store, Germinate and Keep Vegetables,
Plants, Fruits and Herbs Fresh for 5+ Years,
Build Your Own Seed Bank
& Live the Frugal Gardening Lifestyle

By

Steven Dowding

Chapter 1.

LIVE THE FRUGAL GARDENING LIFESTYLE

The economic boom, and the erratic increase of hypermarkets and supermarkets that have settled in the neighborhoods from the extra-urban countryside, have taken away space and clientele from the old shops for a long time.

Thanks to more competitive prices and the possibility of buying (therefore consuming but also wasting) more, the trend towards low-cost food has also affected consumer health.

Finally, the consumers who choose dynamic organic products, zero km, solidarity purchasing, and flavor shops are once again a critical mass and directing the market.

The message of luxury frugality becomes clear: it is better to spend more on quality food, ethically produced for the environment and health, even going so far as to eliminate the extra. Accepting a slightly higher consumer price is equivalent to understanding its greater health, economic and social value.

This is exactly the opinion of seed savers, those who love to get food on their own, grow it and create a self-sustaining system starting from the heart of this thought: the seed.

About forty years ago the movements of seed savers (seed custodians) were born and, with them, a network of gene banks to conserve the seeds of the oldest varieties of food plants (the most famous ones is situated in the Arctic archipelago of Svalbard in Norway). Seed savers were concerned with cultivating, preserving, and storing goods such as vegetables, cereals, and legumes, which in those years — we are at the time of the green revolution, or the advent of the large agri-food industry — they were beginning to disappear.

That's why safeguarding the seeds of your garden allows you to save on purchasing seedlings every year, in addition to the great satisfaction of self-providing. But it is also an act of ecological value when it comes to maintaining ancient varieties that could be lost and conserving biodiversity.

Let's see together how to do it in detail: you, too, can build, step-by-step, your personal seed bank.

Chapter 2.
SEEDS HARVESTING

To better understand how seed savers work and how you can do it too, let's start with an easy example for every beginner and even those curious about this noble art in the name of sustainability: saving tomato seeds.

Tomatoes, in particular, are one of the most cultivated vegetable plants; there are wide varieties: from the classic San Marzano to a myriad of ancient and local varieties.

It is precisely the local cultivars that are most at risk of extinction, which in many cases are preserved only thanks to 'seed savers' who preserve them in their own gardens.

Preserving tomato seeds is an effortless activity and, to do it with good results, you just need a few precautions, which you will find below.

Saving Biodiversity

Buying tomato seedlings would be the most convenient choice: you save time, they are already treated to prevent virus and fungal attacks, and they guarantee a good quantity of fruit. Right? Not really!

The plants purchased generally cannot be defined as completely 'organic': the producers chemically tan the seeds right from the start, and, once germinated, the young tomato seedlings are treated to reduce the risk of disease in the very early stages of life. Furthermore, the advanced genetic techniques applied for years also in agriculture have led to an essential focus on hybrid tomato varieties, i.e., created by laboratory crossings. These are selections resistant to diseases and with specific characteristics in fruit production, but they cannot be reproduced independently.

Without demonizing this practice, we must know that this attitude of the large manufacturing companies is a double-edged sword: by imposing some varieties in place of others, both the importance of biodiversity and the natural adaptation of plants to the surrounding environment are ignored.

Over the years, preserving the seeds through self-production guarantees a tomato cultivar that is increasingly adapted to the climate, the soil, and the water supply available in the geographical area in which it is located. Those who conserve the seeds, therefore, have the possibility of carrying on ancient varieties, often better for the context in which they were developed.

Avoid F1 Hybrid Seeds

When deciding to self-produce seeds, you must consider the nature of the mother plant from which the fruit will be chosen. If you have purchased seedlings that derive from F1 hybrid seeds, it is very probable that weak plants with low productivity will derive from their seeds.

This is because the producers have studied varieties in the laboratory which produce very strong plants in the first generation but which do not maintain the original characteristics with reproduction.

It is easy to understand how the question concerns the mere economic aspect: if everyone could self-produce tomato plants or any other vegetable, the manufacturing companies would get very little from them. By selling the F1 hybrids, the producer remains, in fact, the only owner of the varieties that the buyer must buy every year.

Choose the Right Fruit

To preserve the seeds, you must, first of all, choose the fruit from which to take them. It is a question of identifying a non-hybrid type plant, i.e., with open pollination. Open-pollinated plants are those that have reproduced through natural means such as wind, rain, insects,…

We must therefore look for seeds of a non-hybrid type, to begin with, thus seeds capable of reproducing the same variety of plant. Finding seeds of this type is increasingly difficult, but there are events scattered throughout Italy where passionate greengrocers and industry experts meet to exchange non-hybrid seeds precisely in order to keep alive those varieties that would otherwise disappear. Furthermore, some tomato varieties, such as the Heirloom variety, reproduce only by open pollination, the fruit of which can also be purchased from a trusted greengrocer.

Finally, there are organic seed companies that, by choice, supply non-F1 seeds, such as Arcoiris and Sativa. Obviously, it is recommended to buy seeds from these realities.

Once the pollination has been clarified, we can identify a healthy, robust, vigorous plant and choose some of the most beautiful tomatoes, possibly from the first stages of flowers, i.e., those that develop at the bottom of the plant. Put a ribbon on the chosen fruit just before the stem. This will help you recognize the fruit later in time and not pick it to eat.

To save the seeds, we have to bring the fruit to the maximum point of ripeness, i.e., when the tomato is a very bright red and soft to the touch. In this way, we are guaranteed a seed that will have a high germination index, and we can harvest.

Seed Separation

After having collected the good fruit, we proceed by cutting the tomato in two. Its interior is composed of a soft and gelatinous part, where the seeds are incorporated, and a more solid and spongy part.

With a spoon, we remove the gelatinous part together with the seeds, separating it from the spongy part. Gelatine is composed of a self-germinating substance, which prevents the seed itself from germinating while it is still inside the tomato.

We collect the gelatin and transfer it to an open container, such as a glass or glass bowl. The goal is to remove the gelatin by taking advantage of the fermentation process in the open air.

Fermentation and Pulp Removal

We will have to leave the jelly and seeds to rest in the shade, not too ventilated, for about 3-4 days. After this time, you will notice the formation of a superficial layer of smelly mold. This is the signal that the seeds are ready to be washed and dried.

The seed fermentation process is not essential. However, it reduces the chances of finding yourself with seeds that carry diseases with them because it is a natural sanitization method. Furthermore, the fermentation completely eliminates a germination inhibitor contained in the tomato jelly, which could instead remain even after several washings of the seeds with water.

You have to remove the superficial layer of the mold with a teaspoon, then transfer the remaining jelly into a glass jar, and add clean water and cork.

Washing

At this point, we shake the container to 'wash' the seeds from the jelly. After a few moments, we leave the container to rest. The seeds will sink to the bottom, bringing to the surface the part of the jelly that hasn't gone into solution with the water.

We repeat this operation 2-3 times until the surface of the water in the jar is substantially clear. At this point, transfer the seeds to a colander and pass them under running water for just a few seconds to complete the cleaning cycle. We have obtained our tomato seed.

Seed Drying and Storage

The resulting seeds must be placed on a paper plate or on absorbent paper: the one for bread or fried foods is perfect. Instead, avoid kitchen paper rolls as the seeds, once dry, stick to the paper, making it difficult to remove.

We leave the seeds in the shade, in a slightly ventilated place, for 3-4 days.

Once dried, the seeds should be placed in an airtight container (even a standard glass jar is fine). It is advisable to put them first in a paper bag to be sure to capture even the smallest particles of water left. In fact, it is essential that there is no moisture in the casing to avoid rotting caused by the small parts of water present in the seeds. If this should happen, you are forced to throw away the entire content.

Tomato seeds can also be kept for 4 or 5 years. However, over the years the germinative capacity of the seed decreases, so the best thing is to sow immediately the following season and keep seeds from one year to the next.

We will address this crucial technique in the following Chapters.

Chapter 3.
SEEDS STORING

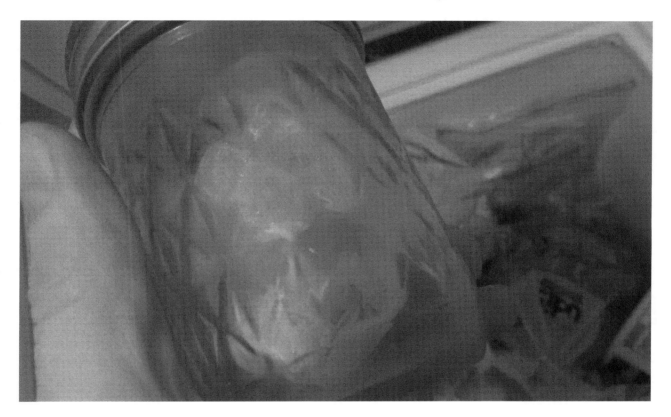

Most of the seeds are harvested with the same techniques that we learned in the tomato example. Similarly, for all types of seeds, the method in which they are stored is a fundamental factor. These are natural products, which have yet to develop, and in order to give their best once planted, they need some special conditions. Otherwise, they can compromise the quantity and quality of the final result.

In this Chapter, you will find the basic rules to follow to store seeds correctly without damaging them and ensure that - after the storage period - they are still in excellent condition, ready to be planted.

Temperature and Humidity

One of the fundamental factors for correct conservation is the temperature, which must necessarily remain below 10 degrees C° (50 F°) to prevent them from activating - thus giving rise to the germination process - in the absence of the right growth conditions. In general, the seeds are able to keep well even with very low temperatures, which is why many growers decide to keep them in the refrigerator or even in the freezer. While this procedure - on the one hand

- does not damage the seeds, which are able to resist up to -20 degrees C° (-4 F°), it puts them in danger because they suffer from humidity. Therefore the defrosting or thawing phase could cause them some damage. If you don't have other tools to lower the temperature, place them in the refrigerator in a dark plastic container with an airtight seal. Avoiding humidity is important: if the seeds are not stored in a dry place, the nutrients present inside will begin to leak, activating the germination phase.

The ideal storage temperature is 4-9 C° (39.2 - 48,2 F°; paying attention also to oscillations), while the humidity should be lower than 35%.

Light and Dark

If light is an indispensable factor for the growth and development of plants, darkness is essential for the correct conservation of the seeds, which prevents the process of germination and development of the seed. For this reason - in addition to the temperature and humidity levels - it is essential to make sure that the seeds are kept in a completely dark environment, just like it also happens for bulbs.

To increase shelf life, in short, it is necessary to remove the seeds from the action of intense light and preserve them from humidity and high temperatures in order to reduce respiratory activity and the consequent consumption of food reserves. Humidity promotes oxidation phenomena which, by causing heating, determine the death of the embryo.

Preservation

Storage must preferably be carried out by dividing the mass of seeds to be stored into small quantities, which must be placed in as many containers as possible. For this purpose, you can use the following:

- Bags made of materials such as jute, cotton, or paper, which are cheap but offer no protection against humidity and rodents;
- Plastic bags of various thicknesses, glass vases, and metal containers, which instead guarantee a high level of defense against humidity and the attack of insects and rodents.

It is always a good idea to label the containers with writing: type of seed, variety, and date of collection.

To prevent insects from multiplying at the expense of the wheat or beans, a frequent stirring of the seeds is recommended. Every day, or almost every day, move the seed container and check its contents, to eliminate all the agents that could damage it.

Tips and Tricks for Proper Seed Storage

- Keep the seeds below 10 °C (50 F°) to prevent them from activating in the absence of ideal conditions.
- The seeds are resistant up to -20°C (-4 F°).

- Keep only seeds obtained from open-pollinated plants.
- Avoid cross-pollination: you can isolate the seedlings by simply placing a nylon bag around the buds, which can be removed as soon as they open.
- Always label your seeds, even if you have a good memory. It will be useful to you.
- Storing the seeds of your plants will help you save money, allowing you to always have a supply of your favorite plant varieties. In short, with a little effort, the advantages will be many.
- After the drying phase, the seeds can be placed in a cellar which however maintains a temperature between 5°C and 10°C (41 - 50 F°) and is not humid.
- Periodically check your seeds and discard any that have rotted or moldy.
- Ideal environmental factors for maintaining them correctly

  - Ideal temperature 4/9°C (39.2 - 48,2 F°);

  - Humidity below 35%;

  - Absolute darkness.

Chapter 4.
SEEDS GERMINATION

Seed germination is an essential process for any agricultural practice: if this does not happen, in fact, we can say goodbye to any idea of crop or plantation we have in mind.

Essential Conditions

To develop and germinate, the seed needs 4 essential conditions:

- Presence of water, i.e., the essential condition for the seed to begin to germinate;
- Presence of oxygen;
- The right temperature, as the seeds, do not germinate below certain temperatures (which vary from species to species, but which are between 15° and 20°); in addition, the temperature also affects the duration of the entire process;
- The right light (we saw it in the previous chapter).

Selection and Scarification

Before proceeding with the actual sowing of the seeds, it is necessary to make a selection of the small seeds that will be planted.

If you choose the crammed ones, it is always good to check the dates: the older the seeds, the less chance they have of germinating.

Furthermore, it is possible that some seeds (by species or by chance) have very stiff integuments, which could make their germination problematic and difficult.

In these cases, a practice called stripping is carried out in order to make the thickness of the casing thinner so as to favor its germination; this can be done in two ways:

- By abrasion;
- By engraving.

With the first method, an abrasive surface (fine-grained sandpaper or nail file) is used to smooth the seed coat, obviously paying close attention not to damage the internal embryo.

The second method recommended to those who are already familiar with this type of practice is carried out by blocking the seed with the fingers or tweezers and incisions it very delicately with a blade on the integument; here, too, we need to take great care not to damage the internal embryo.

If the stripping has been carried out correctly, germination will take place in the right manner and timing.

How Does Seed Germination Occur?

Now that we have a solid foundation on germination, it is time to take action and see how to germinate them.

The techniques are varied, and although there are some general indications, each species has its own peculiarities; the good news is that this practice is absolutely doable and accessible to everyone.

Cotton (or Similar) and Soil

Seed germination, fortunately, is a practice that can be declined in various ways, and this is precisely what makes it within everyone's reach.

Whether you have huge acres of land or a modest terrace, the results you can achieve are equally stunning.

A widespread practice, for example, is to germinate the seeds in cotton (wadding, blotting paper, and gauze are equally good).

The most suitable seeds for this practice are those of legumes such as beans or peas.

The materials needed for this operation are:

- A small container such as a saucer or a glass or plastic cup;

- Cotton wool or cotton pads;
- Seeds.

The procedure is very simple: in fact, it will be enough to put the slightly wet cotton and the seeds spaced a few centimeters apart in the container. In a few days, after constantly watering them with small amounts of water and allowing them to be exposed to light, you will see the first roots sprouting from the cotton. The roots will strengthen and lengthen considerably: this is the signal that the time for potting in the soil has arrived.

After having put a mix of soil and peat in the pot, the seedling must be buried in the center of this, paying particular attention to the roots. This practice, however simple, requires great daily care: the small roots, in fact, could have some difficulty in detaching themselves from the cotton. To avoid this problem, you can think of burying the seeds directly in the soft soil. The golden rule is the following: the seed must be buried to a depth equal to twice its length.

Pro Tips

As we said at the beginning, germination is a very delicate process on which the future of the plant depends. Risky or improvised moves are not useful in these circumstances, but, on the contrary, it is better to have everything under control.

In this section, we give space to some useful advice to put into practice when you notice something anomalous in the germination process.

- The right environment for seed germination - The cultivation environment must be optimal and must, of course, respect the needs of the chosen species: the temperature, humidity, and quality of the soil are variables that must therefore be controlled. PH is also an important variable, and measuring it is an important step for an excellent result.
- Interruption of the growth process - Unfortunately, it sometimes happens that the seedlings start their growth in a normal way, but then there is a sudden interruption of this process. The cause is generally attributable to roots (Pythium, Phytophthora) and molds (Sclerotinia or white mold, Botrytis or gray mold) which destroy the seedling irrecoverably.
- To prevent this condition from occurring, it is good to make sure that the soil is not diseased at the start and to control factors such as temperature and humidity.
- Seeds make no progress in germination - Basically, when the seed does not grow, and the germination process does not go ahead, it is because the seed has not been buried at the right depth, and therefore the roots have no space to grow and develop; another cause may be excessive dryness of the soil and, in this case, just water the plant constantly to solve it.

Seed germination, as you can see, is a delicate and essential process for the survival of our entire ecosystem.

As Kahlil Gibran wrote: 'Civilization began when for the first time man dug the earth and planted a seed.'

Chapter 5.
GERMINATION SECRET HACKS

Have you ever had seeds that just don't want to sprout? Sometimes, there are unsolvable problems that hinder germination. Other times, however, you can go to work to stimulate rapid germination of the seeds.

In this Chapter, we'll look at how to get your seedlings to sprout even when it seems like there's no hope. Sometimes a little heat, humidity, and a lot of passion are enough.

Solid Substrate

To germinate, seeds must be planted somewhere. Even plants grown with hydroponics need a solid substrate, even if minimal. So let's look at three possible substrates for your seeds.

Peat

Among the types of substrate, it is the most used in the professional field. We are talking about peat cubes and/or rock wool, specially designed for the purpose.

Once wet, the peat cubes are soft and airy, ideal for the delicate roots of newborn seedlings. At the same time, they keep the seeds warm and protect them from sudden changes in temperature. When the seedling has grown, to transplant, just take the lump and bury it whole.

Sowing in peat substrate is very easy:

- wet the substrate according to the manufacturer's instructions;
- place the cubes in the jars;
- you create many small holes and bury the seeds;
- pinch the peat to cover the holes.

Earth

The earth is the simplest substrate and is the least traumatic at the time of transplanting: the seedlings don't have to get used to a new habitat, so they recover quite quickly. However, remember that you need very soft and light soil which does not suffocate the newborn roots.

For fast germination, this is the least suitable solution. Even with all its merits, ordinary soil places a barrier between the seeds and the heat source used. On the one hand, this protects them from sudden changes in temperature; on the other, it could weigh them down and delay germination a little.

Blotting Paper

Do you remember when they made you sow lentils in cotton wool or blotting paper at school? Well, you can use this same method, even now that you're an adult, to germinate your seeds. This is a simple technique:

- overlap 10 sheets of blotting paper;
- moisten them all with water or chamomile infusion, which stimulates germination;
- lay the seeds on the surface;
- once the seedlings have sprouted, cut the absorbent paper and plant it together with the seedlings.

The advantage of blotting paper is that you can follow the germination of the seeds step by step. The disadvantage is that the seeds lack protection and nourishment: as soon as the first two leaves appear, you must immediately transplant them.

Build a Grow-Box

For fast seed germination, choosing a substrate is just the beginning. In fact, the rapid germination of the seeds needs heat and humidity: if it is too cold, the seeds do not awaken; if the environment is too dry, the integument remains rigid, and the bud cannot break it. A grow box is a small greenhouse designed for seeds and newborn plants.

The simplest solution is to buy a ready-made grow box. Otherwise, you can do it yourself starting from these materials:

- a box with a lid 40cm high for a mini grow box, 80cm for a larger grow box;
- aluminum foil;
- a heating mat, especially if your house is cold;
- an LED lamp to be placed on top of the box;
- containers with substrate and seeds.

Line the box with aluminum foil and drill two small holes in it for the cables to pass through. Insert the mat, the seed containers, and the lamp, then wait. Like greenhouses, grow boxes also need periodic air circulation. Ready-made kits include a small ventilation system.

Chapter 6.
BUILD YOUR OWN SEED BANK

The need to conserve is inherent in our human nature, but instead of preserving money and objects with that form of attachment which then leads to the inexorable anguish of losing them, we could start conserving seeds.

Seeds cannot be stored for decades, some last longer, others less, but all sooner or later must be planted and reproduced; after all, the best seed bank is the earth!

For this reason, a seed bank should be dynamic and open, without fear of entrusting even the most precious seeds, provided they are given to people capable of reproducing them.

When we talk about seed banks, many think of that of Svalbard, in Norway, where under the ice and the stone, immense quantities of germplasm are conserved for the good of humanity decades after decades; few know, however, that this type of bank can be financed and supported by the same people who are destroying the planet!

Also, for this reason, local seed banks, managed by knowledgeable people and by seed savers, are an essential resource for farmers, breeders, and also for all consumers.

The natural seeds (those that you throw to the ground and grow and bear fruit by themselves or almost) are slowly replaced by ad hoc hybridized seeds that meet the industrial reproduction criteria. Therefore they need more water, they do not know how to defend themselves from parasites, they are food supplied by us, and in general, they don't know how to manage independently!

Maintaining biodiversity in the species that populate the earth guarantees a more varied and healthier diet and a faster response to environmental disasters.

The traditional seed savers, i.e., the 'old' farmers of the past, are slowly disappearing. They haven't been replaced in at least two generations. But something is changing: and the fact that you are reading these pages is the most evident proof.

Preserving local species gives us a more varied and beautiful world: now that you know how to do it, here are some tips for creating your own personal seed bank.

With an important caveat: don't keep it to yourself! Spread your knowledge and skills, interact with the world's seed-saver networks (start from those in your region, without worries) and help save the culture of sustainable biodiversity.

Let's go!

- The fundamental rule is always to know your limits and your available resources. Don't do or give more than you can or have, not out of selfishness but because then you need time to recover, blocking - and sometimes losing - the work done. Or you may become a heavy person because you are too empty and tired.
- For an informal bank, you need a cool, dry place, paper, or airtight containers, depending on the seeds, labels, and good cataloging skills.
- Then you collect the seeds that you have, that they bring you, and that you find, making sure that they are dry and trying in some way to verify if the seed is actually what they tell you it is. Sometimes it happens to me that they give me the seeds of a plant, mistaking it for another.
- Catalog them by clearly writing the name, place, year, and if they have particular characteristics.
- Put yourself out there, giving a name to the project, and then spread as much as possible. People will come to you like flies to honey; for my part, I have received great empathy, and many share this desire to save our future.
- I have the possibility of organizing information desks and sending seeds by post, but you could also just make yourself available for those who want to pick up the seeds directly from you. You can leave them at a strategic point in the village or where you live, or you can ask friends to help you with deliveries.
- The important thing, I repeat, is not to feel forced to do anything, to put passion into it, and to set a good example.

Best Vegetables for Your Seedbank

Even if most horticultural crops can be grown in seedbeds, it is necessary to know that some species do not tolerate transplanting, so it is good to know which crops are suitable for sowing in trays.

- All cucurbits lend themselves very well to transplanting: pumpkin, courgette, melon, watermelon, and cucumber. The technique is also valid for peppers, hot peppers, aubergines, tomatoes, head lettuce, chard, celery, cabbage, and other vegetables.
- In general, those species that are placed at well-defined distances in the garden are transplanted, while it would be less convenient for species that are placed in a continuous row, such as rocket and parsley or peas and beans, because in this way, too many seedlings would be needed and therefore you might as well do direct sowing in rows. However, some farms do the transplantation of rocket, spinach, and parsley, because with direct sowing in rows, the rapid birth of weeds would then make it challenging to keep the row clean, and therefore, they prefer to transplant the tufts of 3-4 seedlings on the black perforated sheets.
- For carrots, turnips, and radishes, transplanting is not recommended because it is difficult for the seedlings to take root. Being root species, moreover, direct sowing in the garden is better in order to obtain more regular and good-sized vegetables.
- If we have little space for the seedbed, we have to make a choice between the seedlings to sow and those to buy. In this case, it is preferable to purchase leek and onion seedlings because they are placed in the garden at short distances, and many are needed: we would risk investing all our small seedbed space only with these.
- Furthermore, the seeds of leeks and onions can be kept for a maximum of 2 years, so if there are leftover sachets that are opened, they could expire before they are entirely used.

BOOK 7

Make Money

with Excess Vegetables:

Sell Surplus Vegetables,
Monetize Your Hard Work,
Build an Additional Stream of Income,
and Make Infinite ROI

By

Steven Dowding

Chapter 1.
SMALL IS BEAUTIFUL (AND PROFITABLE)

Everywhere in the world, there is a general awareness of the serious consequences of industrial agriculture: pesticides, GMOs, cancer, the agri-food industry, etc. This awareness has translated into a general enthusiasm for organic, healthy, and local agriculture.

However, when you think of farms, old-fashioned farmers, and seed savers, you have an almost 'bucolic' conception of the whole thing: people living on the fringes of society making a basic livelihood. This is completely unfounded!

On the contrary, it is possible to create mini-farms that are organized and capable of making very significant income. To convince you that small is beautiful but also very profitable, I'll tell you my personal experience.

Thanks to the possibility of using various forms of marketing, today, there is an important niche for small-scale agriculture, and there are concrete opportunities for many young people (and not) to move to the countryside and make agriculture their source of income.

So, I started my farming career with a very small garden, selling vegetables at local farmers' markets.

I had rented a small piece of land of 1000 square meters where my family and I were temporarily camping for the summer. It didn't take a large investment in terms of tools and equipment to get started. The fact of being rented has prompted us to limit expenses in order to cover the management costs with our business and set aside enough money to invest, get through the winter and make some trips. At the time, we were happy just to grow and make ends meet!

Then came the moment when we felt the need to settle down somewhere. We needed security, a desire to build our own home, and to put down roots in our small community. This new beginning meant that our garden should generate enough income to overcome the costs of the land, the needs of the family, and the construction of the house.

Instead of mechanizing our cultivation operations, following the path of more conventional horticulture, I thought it would be possible, if not preferable, to intensify my production but continue to work mostly by hand. My principle was to produce better rather than produce more. With this idea in mind, I set out to research horticultural techniques and tools that would make growing vegetables on a small scale more efficient and profitable.

In the end, our research and our discoveries, the result of many experiences, have allowed us to create a productive and profitable horticultural micro-company.

Every week my garden supplies more than 200 families and generates an income high enough to live with dignity.

The initial strategy, which consisted of creating a 'low-tech' system, made it possible to limit the initial start-up costs, and so my company had already become profitable after only a few years of activity. Our management fees are always quite low, so much so that I haven't had any economic difficulties so far. On the other hand, like when I started, my main activity is farming, and, despite all the changes taking place within the company, our lifestyle has always remained the one we had chosen at the beginning. The farm works for us and not the other way around!

Along the way, we called ourselves 'gardeners-horticulturists' to underline our choice to work with hand tools. Unlike conventional horticulturists, we do not cultivate fields, but gardens, limiting the use of fossil fuels as much as possible. All of our activities - high productivity in a small area, the use of intensive production methods, the use of techniques to extend the seasonality of products and direct sales to city markets - are inspired by the French horticultural tradition, though our practices have at the same time been influenced by our American neighbors.

That said, I'm not suggesting that the mechanization of farming operations should be banned. After all, the best horticultural farms that I have visited over time were often highly mechanized.

My point of view is rather the following: the use of a farm tractor and other mechanical tools to weed and till the soil does not necessarily lead to more profitable horticultural practices. Non-mechanization or the use of alternative machineries, such as a professional rotary cultivator, on the other hand, has several advantages to take into consideration, especially when starting out.

Living with Just One Hectare

Most experts in the world of agriculture welcome the possibility of making a profit from a horticultural micro-company, or professional garden, as we call it, with clear skepticism. It is possible that they will try to discourage those of you who want to start a project similar to ours. Not to worry too much because mentalities are changing as micro-agriculture in the United States, Japan, and other parts of the world is demonstrating the impressive potential of artisanal production that operates within channels of local distribution.

In my first year of operation, the farm made $20,000 in product sales, with a quarter-acre plot under cultivation.

The following year, our sales raised $55,000, still growing the same acreage.

In our third year of business, we invested in new equipment and moved onto the land we were cultivating.

Expanding the area planted to three-quarters of an acre, our sales reached $80,000, then $100,000 in our fourth season. At this point, our micro-farm had achieved a level of production and economic success that most agricultural experts believed impossible.

When we made our turnover public, in the context of competition for agricultural companies, our company received important recognition for its excellent economic performance!

I also know many other small producers who manage to make a good income from their small intensive farming business. This model is profitable; it's proven!

Furthermore, it is also legitimate to think that you can get a rather high income from it. An established professional garden with a well-developed production plan and good sales channels can generate between $60,000 and $120,000 in sales annually with less than an acre of mixed vegetables and a profit margin of over 40%. %. A net income that can easily be compared to many other agricultural sectors.

Earn a Living, Living Well

The idea that most people have about our profession is that we are obsessed with people who work seven days a week, non-stop, to barely earn enough to survive. An idea that is probably based on the real problems of most conventional farmers trapped in the grip of modern agriculture.

It is true that the job of a horticulturist is sometimes difficult. Come rain or shine; we are always subject to the vagaries of unpredictable weather. Exceptional harvests and good years are never a guarantee, and a good dose of courage and commitment is needed, especially in the first years of activity, when a clientele and the necessary infrastructures have yet to be built.

Nonetheless, it is an extraordinary profession, characterized not so much by working hours or wages but rather by the quality of life it offers. Few can imagine it, but despite the intensity of our work, we still have tons of time left to devote to other things.

Our season starts gradually in March and ends in December. That's a total of nine months of work and three months of vacation. Winter is a precious time to rest, travel or do any other activity.

To all those who think we are doing a starvation job, I would like to answer that our business allows us to live in the countryside, to reconcile work and family within a natural environment, and to have guaranteed employment, unlike employees in a large company, where layoffs are unpredictable and frequent. This is a considerable advantage.

Chapter 2.
VEGETABLES OF ABUNDANCE

Opening a farm is your dream, but you have a thousand questions buzzing in your head - first of all, how profitable you can be and generate infinite ROI by selling excess vegetables - and you don't know where to start? Let's see how to get things done.

According to the National Agricultural Statistics Service Census of Agriculture, family farms are 96 percent of the more than 2 million farms in the United States. Therefore, family farms must indeed be doing something right, for there are so many of them! Beyond the innate spirit of farms that equates to 'familiarity,' generational collaboration also offers a number of benefits.

First, family farms tend to be smaller, which leads to higher quality produce, benefiting the economy and the environment in equal measure. How? Smaller farms are often more productive on a day-to-day basis than large industrial farms, simply due to the level of production per unit of land. This significantly reduces energy and water consumption while maintaining the level of food production needed to feed an ever-growing population.

Family farms are also more likely to maintain traditional processes, from raising livestock to growing a variety of plants, all of which are incredibly beneficial to ecosystems.

Furthermore, there is much to be said about the way family businesses help maintain cultural values: the importance of family, trust, and community. These companies also ensure family members - and others - a guaranteed job in a world where unemployment and poverty have reached devastating levels. In short, family farms provide that no one is left behind.

So let us begin our journey on how to start an agricultural business, whether it is to open a family farm, an organic farm, or become a young agricultural entrepreneur.

How much Land Do I Need?

To understand how much land is needed to open a farm, first of all, you need to understand what type of crop you want to grow.

Keep in mind that each crop has specific soil requirements. Depending on the characteristics of the land and its extension, you will be able to make a targeted choice on what to cultivate.

Bottom line: DO NOT start a farm by investing all your money in the land!

What is Best to Grow in My Land?

Some crops are pretty tolerant of soil characteristics, while others are susceptible. Before starting your business as an agricultural entrepreneur, you need to take a soil sample because it provides crucial information on its nature (for example, PH value, humus content, micro-macroelement endowment, etc.).

Taking a sample is recommended not only because you understand how fertile or tired your soil is, but it can also help you make the right choice in the type of crop to be planted and will subsequently help you choose a targeted fertilization method.

Bottom line: DO NOT open a farm without knowing your land thoroughly! The principal capital of the farmer is the land itself. The plants are a consequence.

Should I Have Direct Access to Water for Irrigation?

The possibility of irrigating plants is the fundamental prerequisite for the professional cultivation of almost all crops. The amount of water you need for your crops and the frequency with which you will irrigate depend not only on the harvest and the phases of the vegetative cycle but also on the characteristics of your soil, its morphology, and climatic conditions.

What Tools or Machines? How Much Should I Spend?

Every agricultural activity requires the use of machines to work the soil and take measures to protect the crops and plants, as well as possibly for harvesting. All this translates into costs and various fixed expenses for the farm. However, inter-company use of machines supplied by so-called contractors is often used, so it is not necessary to immediately buy expensive machinery such as tractors, plows, sprayers, etc. However, you need to ensure there is someone in your area who can provide them for you.

Furthermore, it is necessary to calculate possible investments in the conservation, marketing, and processing of agricultural products.

Can I Based My Farm Only On Incentives and Contributions?

Any incentives for opening the farm are to be considered as initial support for the start-up, but this economic reserve must not be decisive in your decision to open or not a farm.

Consider that the agricultural world is not all rosy! Unforeseen events are around the corner and of various kinds (adverse climatic events such as drought, frost, floods, market downturns, etc.).

However, we cannot rely solely on 'external' or one-off grants. To devote yourself to agriculture as a professional, you need to have a good dose of preparation in the field, motivation, constant commitment, personal initiative, and interest. If you are not an expert, therefore, it is still advisable to study a lot and rely on the advice of expert people, local but also similar to you, who have gone through this experience before you.

A Passing of Legacy

The tradition of family-run farms is also essential for the final passing of the baton: from the older generations to the younger ones.

Young people's interest in farming is vital to the future of farming, and family farms are the ideal way to inspire and engage young people to pursue a career in this industry, following in their ancestor's footsteps.

However, this future is not without its challenges. To continue to thrive, smaller and family-owned businesses must compete with industry giants while also dealing with the impact of social, economic, and climate change.

Chapter 3.
12 SMALL IN MANAGEMENT BUSINESS, BIG IN TURNOVER

I f we have already highlighted in the previous chapters how to give life to your mini-farm, homesteading, and business, let's now see the 12 most profitable sectors related to the world of small family-run agricultural enterprises. Small in management, big in turnover.

Because the possibility of earning money with your land does exist, but let's not make it too easy. Before launching yourself into the enterprise (which I suggest you approach, at least at the beginning, as a simple hobby), you will need to make all the necessary assessments. And gather helpful information to make you understand if your' handkerchief of land' can actually yield something in all senses.

Mushrooms

The cultivation of mushrooms is a market that knows no crisis; this is why starting cultivation could prove to be a winning idea. But where to start? First of all, the substrate must be prepared to implant the mycelia, which are nothing but the vegetative apparatus of the mushrooms.

There are those who enrich it with wood shavings, but much more widespread is the practice that involves the use of straw (which is broken up and suitably moistened), manure, chalk, and hay. The compound obtained must 'rest' for two weeks at a temperature of about 25° C, thus allowing the mycelium to grow inside it. And then? It is necessary to cover the substrate with particular soil and wait for another ten days. Until the actual reproductive phase is reached, during which the ambient temperature must be lowered to about 18° C. By committing oneself to respect times and temperatures and guaranteeing the right level of acidity in the soil, the first mushrooms will appear after about a week. Let them grow a little longer, and use them as you wish.

Aloe Vera

Aloe vera has become a real trend, which involves both the cosmetic and food markets. What are we talking about? Of a semi-fat plant which - according to experts - has significant beneficial effects on our health (soothing, purifying, protective, and strengthening) and which, precisely, for this reason, can represent a good source of income.

However, those who are thinking of growing aloe vera must know that having land available may not be enough because aloe is a plant that grows in warm areas and needs a lot of suns. Since it can also be planted in uneven terrain and does not require much water, the costs for starting an aloe vera cultivation are relatively low also because we are talking about a plant that does not require particular maintenance but watches out for ants who risk spoiling your party if they get to the leaves.

Goji Berries

Consuming Goji berries has also become an actual customer for a growing number of Italians. Who could think of starting, on their land, the cultivation of Goji berries, originally from Tibet and China, which gives fruits with recognized antioxidant properties?

To carry out the project, then, it is necessary to have well-drained and fertilized medium-textured soil (preferably slightly acidic). And then you need to arm yourself with patience because, from the moment of 'sowing' to that of the first flowering and fruiting, it will take two years. However, we are talking about a crop that does not require particular maintenance (just guaranteeing it the right amount of water and the proper exposure to light), with the exception of pruning. In fact, Goji berries bear fruit only on young branches. Therefore, it is advisable to periodically eliminate the old ones, which risks compromising their growth.

Saffron

We say it right away: growing saffron requires an economic effort, but it can also guarantee good income. It is, in fact, very expensive due to the particular maintenance it requires. Where should you start? From the planting of the bulbs, which, according to the testimony of those who have already embarked on the enterprise, it would be good to place in hilly terrain (not clayey). The best time to sow is between July and August, which allows you to harvest in

December. The saffron plant – which needs lots of light and a small amount of water to grow (stagnation can cause the bulbs to rot) – produces beautiful purple flowers, which are open, however, only for a few days. It is in this short period of time that it is necessary to operate, being careful to handle with care the stigmas from which the spice is obtained. It is, in fact, a very delicate operation that can only be carried out by 'insiders.'

Lavender

Who doesn't love the scent of lavender freshening up their laundry drawers? What if you tried to grow lavender on your land instead of buying it already packaged and marketed?

The idea could prove to be a happy one, but as always, various factors must be taken into consideration. Being a Mediterranean plant (the most flourishing plantations are found in Provence, France), it needs well-drained, sufficiently clayey, and sandy soil. It has a temperate climate, with hot summers and mild winters, with very low humidity. As for maintenance, remember that the lavender plant must be pruned after flowering. And that once the flowers have been collected, they must be dried in a closed, cool, and shady place, which guarantees the maintenance of the characteristic fragrance. If things go well, you can start a small business. Or limit yourself to giving the 'fruits' of your harvest to a small circle of friends and relatives.

Snail Breeding

Although the term can easily mislead, the cultivation of snails is a business that, since 2004, has known no obstacles. On the contrary, it has been in perennial and constant growth, regardless of any global economic and financial crises. Its great success derives mostly from the discovery of ancient gastronomic traditions at a local and regional level.

The initial investment for starting a snail farm is quite demanding: we are talking about figures ranging from 20,000 to 30,000 euros. The reason for this figure? Very simple. To leave, it is necessary to have large land available. In fact, "only" 20/25 snails manage to grow within a square meter. In addition to purchasing the plot (if you don't already own one), you will also need to provide valuable machinery for working the land. And, of course, also the construction of fences that serve to separate the tiny breeding snails from the snails that you will fatten. Not to mention the irrigation system to keep the earth consistently moist. Do not forget that the turnover, in fact, develops with the sale of live animals. One of the pluses of growing snails certainly concerns the time factor. All it takes is 18 hours a week of commitment, and that's in addition to that very romantic aspect that involves reconciling with nature and recovering one's outdoor spaces outside the walls of the house and far from the inputs of technology.

Educational Farm

The educational farm is a reality that has had enormous success over the last few years. It is mostly a farm that organizes academic courses for children and school groups of different ages. But also for adults who love nature and are curious to find out what country life is like. The company takes care of promoting and organizing days dedicated to the explanation and demonstration of what happens on the farm. From animal husbandry to vegetable gardening. From fruit and vegetable picking to cheese making. In reality, the educational farm is nothing more than a farm (or a farmhouse) that opens its doors to the public, showing them everyday life. It is an interesting opportunity both as a form of income and as a proposal to promote one's services and the sale of one's products.

Bamboo

We have all heard of bamboo before. Yet many of us don't know that this plant is one of the most used to beautify gardens. Did you know that this particular variety of potted trees can also be sold for more than 100 euros? Not bad, right? Very often, bamboo is associated with Japan, but, in reality, this plant can grow well even in areas with colder temperatures. Try to find out from the nursery closest to your home to find out which variety grows best in your area to start your bamboo cultivation.

Ginseng

Ginseng is one of the traditional crops of China. Already present for thousands of years in the land of the Rising Sun, in recent years, it has also arrived in Europe and Italy, conquering many people with its taste and its properties. It is one of the most promising crops on our continent. However, some clarifications need to be made regarding the growth and sale of this plant. In fact, ginseng takes six years to develop from a simple seed to a mature tree with its leaves. During this period, however, you will be able to start making your first earnings through the sale of the seeds but also of the roots. According to some recent estimates, an acre of land used entirely for the cultivation of ginseng can generate earnings of up to 100.00 euros.

Medicinal and Officinal Herbs

Medicinal and officinal herbs are part of that category of crops that do not require particular plots of land. On the contrary, even spaces with no exaggerated dimensions can suffice. Their seeds can be purchased both online and at nurseries near your home and have meager prices. Through the sale of these plants (but also their flowers or leaves), it is possible to obtain cosmetic products, essential oils, and herbal teas. Furthermore, some of them can also be used in the kitchen for the creation of tasty and very fragrant dishes.

Beekeeping

Honey is part of that type of natural product that is particularly appreciated in the kitchen. But it is also often used as a natural remedy for seasonal ailments such as coughs, colds, and flu. Perhaps not everyone knows, however, that around 4,000 tons of this food are exported a year in our country alone. We must not forget, however, that when we speak of beekeeping, we are not referring only to the production of honey but also to that of royal jelly, propolis, and beeswax.

In the event that this type of activity should interest you, but you are a perfect neophyte in the sector, we advise you to take a unique beekeeper course, which is very useful for learning how to manage a beehive in complete tranquility and safety. And, above all, to avoid being victims of unpleasant accidents or unpleasant experiences. The best land in which to start your own beekeeping business is the one rich in flowers. It would also be ideal if it were located in an area not too exposed to the wind and whose slope is not very pronounced. Among the start-up costs, you will have to include the purchase of hives, i.e., bee houses. But also finding a protective suit that covers your entire face and body. In principle, the initial investment can be around 1500 euros. A figure that cannot be considered absolutely excessive.

Finally, to recover the bees, you have two options. The first is to recover them in the wild (this is a procedure that takes quite a bit of time). The second is to buy one or more colonies from some bee breeders in your area (faster and more practical, especially for those who are not so expert in the sector).

Vegetable Garden for Rent

A rented vegetable garden can prove to be an excellent solution for those who have a relatively large plot of land at their disposal but don't particularly want time or passion to keep up with it. Through this option, you will have the possibility to rent the whole field or parts of it to other people who want to use it for growing vegetables themselves. Alternatively, you can consistently offer the families in the area to give you a small amount a month to grow the vegetables they want for them. You can expect to be paid from $0.20 to $2.50 per square foot of garden space (U.S. data). That is $20 to $250 for a 100-square-foot plot, the equivalent to a 10 feet x 10 feet square space.

You can make a list of vegetables to make available and then make it available to potential customers. In this way, you will be paid to cultivate the land, and you will have the opportunity to make the most of your garden and earn a little more, which doesn't hurt.

Starting one of these crops on your private land, perhaps combining it with the sowing of vegetables and flowers, could give you great well-being.

Do not underestimate the idea, and if you feel sufficiently inspired and motivated to ride it, ask for advice from those who have already embarked on the path of 'green' entrepreneurship. Networking – also in this case – can help you a lot.

Chapter 4.
MAKE MONEY WITH EXCESS VEGETABLES: BEST HACKS

E-commerce will be the nerve center of your business. Here are some hacks to make it better:

- pay attention to the naming to which you will link your online presence;
- prepare complete and exhaustive product sheets;
- do not underestimate the aesthetics and seaworthiness;
- provide information content that tells the whole chain of your products, organic and otherwise;
- leave room for reviews;
- make sure that the purchasing system is fully functional and that there is all the information on shipments and the rights of withdrawal;
- don't forget to make your data management policy clear;
- you can also integrate a blog where you will tell about your company and write ad hoc articles on products or cultivation methods; it is essential that the blog is managed with particular attention to SEO in order to be indexed easily on search engines.

This can then be communicated in several ways:

- through inbound marketing, such as the blog and the relaunch of quality articles on social networks;
- through social media advertising;
- through contacts with influencers who are particularly attentive and interested in food or organic issues.

Selling Vegetables: Other Solutions

If all this seems too complicated or beyond your financial means, you can always 'go traditional,' based on the sharing economy and face-to-face relationships.

Wholesale and Retail

When it comes to wholesale, we get scared because we always think of supermarkets: in reality, we can include other less demanding (at least economically) realities such as local cooperatives, general markets, or merchants in this category. However, I feel like telling you these are ways to go once the company is very structured and large.

My advice is this: stay small! Yes, I may seem unambitious, perhaps, but I assure you that in farming, you have more profit margin, lower expenses, better management of your work, and certainly a little more time for yourself if you stay within the family size. Oh, I forgot: definitely fewer problems!

At this point, therefore, retail is the most suitable and profitable solution for a small farm that can still turn to restaurants, small fruit and vegetable shops, weekly markets, and direct sales.

Direct Selling

This is the type of sale that I have chosen given the small size of my company, and I assure you it is an excellent system. In fact, you can carry out direct sales either at your farm, as I do, or by moving to local markets or both. The choice is absolutely personal but dictated by very specific stakes; In fact, while for sale on the farm, you just need to equip yourself with a counter, a scale, some other accessory for sale, and a sheltered place to carry it out, well, to sell on markets you need all this plus a van or in any case a suitable vehicle for transporting vegetables (perhaps wet) and above all it takes time!

Not insignificant if you think that your time still has a cost and subtracting it from crops could become harmful. So let's say that this solution is suitable for those who have time and people available.

Direct sales in the company, as I do, is always the best way to go, in my opinion, and even carried out in an integral way by selling only exclusive products that you grow without buying them elsewhere.

I assure you that the effort in growing, packaging, and then selling your vegetables can be found in the compliments of the customers as much as in the economic aspect of the raw sale.

Being told by whoever covers your carrots that he has rediscovered the flavors of the past, rather than being surprised by the taste of tomatoes or salads because he didn't even remember them, or even saying, 'finally, this strawberry tastes like strawberry,' repays you for your efforts newspapers; here are these satisfactions a trader will never be able to try them.

Summing Up

You need constancy and commitment every day; you need seriousness and honesty. This is what the customer looks for from you! Elsewhere one can find everything at perhaps lower prices, but they don't always find these virtues; I assure you that in the long run, your results will come even economically.

The economic yield is clearly determined, but in agriculture, it is difficult, I would say impossible, to estimate it!

However, you have different ways to start earning with your garden: choose the one that best suits you based on how many vegetables you grow, the time spent in your garden or in your garden, and above all, your work goals.

Remember: the world of online sales can be very useful whether you are already an entrepreneur in the fruit and vegetable sector or if you take care of your garden as a hobby.

Good luck!

CONCLUSION: YOUR PERSONAL TOUCH

This wonderful journey into the sustainable, beautiful, and profitable world of self-sufficient vegetable gardens comes to an end. I hope that, by reading this book, you will be motivated even more to carry out your project!

Reread it several times, as it is full of very useful advice that will help you design not only a vegetable garden but a really profitable and modern farm.

And to do that, you'll need to let the topics settle, study them several times and, of course, start putting them into practice!

Be curious and creative, and always put your touch on it: in fact, without innovation and creativity, it is difficult to compete in the market because the competition is very prepared and competitive.

The modern agricultural entrepreneur is no longer just a man who has chosen the countryside but a professional capable of moving in the most varied fields, from land to the internet.

A figure with many professionalisms who care not only about their survival but, above all, that of the planet in its most natural essence without superstructures.

If your dream is to start a zero km organic vegetable garden, this book will become your most faithful ally!

As we're winding down, I would love to read your honest review on Amazon... I can't wait to hear your thoughts and your story about it!

Happy reading and have a wonderful experience,

Steven

Made in United States
Troutdale, OR
05/31/2023

10356406R00096